T0209901

Promise You Won't Get Mad

And Other Read-Aloud Plays for Young People

Amy K. Rider

Routledge
Taylor & Francis Group

NEW YORK AND LONDON

First published in 2000 by Prufrock Press Inc.

Published 2021 by Routledge
605 Third Avenue, New York, NY 10017
2 Park Square, Milton Park, Abingdon, Oxon OX14 4RN

Routledge is an imprint of the Taylor & Francis Group, an informa business

ISBN 13: 978-1-877673-39-9 (pbk)

This is for my mom, Sharon Rider, and in memory of my grandparents, John and Viola Rider.

Everybody has a story.

Table of Contents
and
Synopses

It's Not a Party— It's a Get-Together!

CHARACTERS

Narrator #1
Narrator #2
Mr. Warren
Mrs. Warren
Mr. Anderson
Mrs. Anderson

Students (male):
  Brian
  Luke
  Kyle
  Casey

Students (female):
  Justine
  Trina
  Bethany
  Elaine
  Jennifer
  Kelly

Narrator #1: It is Thursday afternoon. School is out for the day, and several students are wandering around the mall. One of them, Brian, is clearly excited about his plans for the coming weekend.

Brian: I can't believe what a genius I am! Luke, did you ever realize you had a genius for a friend?

Luke: No . . . and I'm still not sure I do.

Brian: What do you mean you're not sure? I'm brilliant. Who else could come up with a plan this great? What am I even doing wandering around this stupid mall? I should be in medical school or something.

Justine: Before you start sending out applications, could you explain this great plan of yours to me? I haven't heard it yet.

Trina: I heard it, but it's kind of confusing.

Brian: Everything is confusing to you, Trina.

TRINA: Not math.

BRIAN: Well, everything else.

TRINA: Not science.

BRIAN: You know what I mean. Everything *real*.

BETHANY: Maybe she just doesn't have the mind of a criminal, Brian.

BRIAN: (*Sounding angry*) Are you calling me a dirty, rotten criminal?

BETHANY: No. I'm just saying you *think* like one.

BRIAN: Oh. Well, I guess that's all right.

TRINA: Isn't anyone going to explain this thing?

LUKE: I'll explain it. Not that I think like a criminal or anything . . . because I don't. I even tried to pay extra for my lunch today when the cook accidentally gave me three rolls instead of two.

ELAINE: (*Impatient*) Just tell us the plan, all right? Otherwise I'm going to go try on some shoes.

LUKE: Okay. My parents are going out of town Saturday night. They're going to stay at this really cool hotel next to an amusement park. (*Dramatically*) Of course, since the hotel is next to an amusement park, I begged them to take me with them, along with a friend. But do you think they care what their only son has to say? Did they ever even think that maybe I need to get away, too? My life is full of stress. The way things are going, I'm probably going to have a heart attack before I get my driver's license, and they act like they're the ones who—

JUSTINE: Would you please get to the point? The mall closes in five hours, you know.

LUKE: Okay, okay. Anyway, they're practically abandoning me to go off on their own, and so I'm staying overnight at Brian's—

BRIAN: And here's where my plan comes in.

LUKE: Hey, I was telling it.

BRIAN: Sorry, Luke. You're just taking too long. (*To the others*) Luke's supposed to stay at my place because his parents don't want him to be alone in the apartment over-night, right? Well, he won't be alone, but he won't be at my house, either. Luke and I are staying at his place. We're telling my parents that Luke's parents cancelled their plans and we're going to stay at his place instead.

TRINA: But won't Luke's parents check with your parents?

JUSTINE: Or won't your parents get suspicious?

BRIAN: Why should they? We've been staying overnight with each other for years.

LUKE: They trust us. There is very little chance they are going to talk to each other.

JUSTINE: My parents would check.

TRINA: Mine, too.

LUKE: Ours won't, okay? Can we get on with the story?

TRINA: Okay, okay.

BRIAN: So anyway, we're going to have the whole place to ourselves. If you guys are nice, we may even invite you over.

ELAINE: Luke, isn't there a swimming pool in your apartment complex? Should I forget about those shoes and start looking for a swimsuit?

LUKE: No way. Don't even think about buying new clothes for this because we're definitely not . . .

ELAINE: (Interrupting him) Don't worry, Luke. It wouldn't just be for this weekend. I've been needing a new suit, anyway.

LUKE: No, that's not what I mean. We're not having anyone over.

BRIAN: (Surprised) What are you saying? We have to have people over.

JUSTINE: Don't you watch TV, Luke? Or go to the movies? Every time the parents go out of town and leave their kid home alone, the kid throws a huge party.

ELAINE: It's normal, Luke. You've always been normal . . . Well, pretty normal.

LUKE: Yes, but technically my parents aren't leaving me home alone. They're sending me to Brian's.

BETHANY: Do you always have to miss the point?

LUKE: No . . . but maybe this time I did.

JUSTINE: The point is, you're going to have the whole place . . .

ELAINE: . . . and a pool, too.

BRIAN: Look at it this way. Kids are supposed to do stuff like this. Adults expect it. Otherwise their lives would be way too dull. They depend on us to keep them from dying of boredom.

ELAINE: See! It's normal.

BRIAN: If it weren't for us, adults would just go to work all the time and then come home and talk about all the bills they have to pay. You practically owe it to your parents to have all your friends over when they're not there.

JUSTINE: Yes, they're probably going out of town just so you can do this.

BRIAN: Besides, your parents will never even know about it.

LUKE: How will it keep them from dying of boredom then if they don't even know about it?

BETHANY: (To Brian) There he goes again, missing the point.

It's Not a Party—It's a Get-Together!

LUKE: But in those movies, where the kid has a party, something always gets broken. What if that happens?

ELAINE: Haven't you ever heard of super glue? That's what they use in the movies.

LUKE: What if it's not something you can glue? What if it's a curtain or something?

ELAINE: A needle and thread then.

TRINA: Maybe we ought to think about this. What if his parents do find out about it? What if they come home early or something?

JUSTINE: Oh, please, Trina. That only happens in the movies.

NARRATOR #2: Later that afternoon, the students are waiting outside the mall for their parents to pick them up. They are still talking about the party.

ELAINE: It really wouldn't have to be a *party*, Luke. You could just have some people over.

LUKE: But that would make it a party, wouldn't it?

BETHANY: No way. A party is where you have really loud, booming music and a 150 people screaming and shouting and dancing around.

CASEY: Yes, Luke. You couldn't have a party even if you wanted to. I've seen your parents' stereo.

BETHANY: And you don't even *know* 150 people.

JUSTINE: You barely know 10 people.

CASEY: It's not like you're popular or anything. If you were, then you might have a problem. But you're not. You hardly know anyone, so there's nothing to worry about.

ELAINE: Actually, you're really lucky not to be popular. If it was at my house, I'd have to invite at least 150 people. Probably more.

LUKE: (*Offended*) Hey, I know a lot of people. I could have a party if I wanted to.

BRIAN: But it won't be a party, anyway. It's just a get-together. Just a few friends sitting around watching TV.

LUKE: Hmmmmmm . . . it's just a get-together then—even though I could have a party if I wanted to . . . because I know plenty of people. And by the way, my parents' stereo isn't that bad.

ELAINE: Right. So it will just be a few people at the get-together.

BRIAN: Exactly. Just a few people . . .

TRINA: So how many is that?

ELAINE: I think it's about seven.

BRIAN: Well, that means you can't come then.

ELAINE: Actually, I think it's eight.

LUKE: Maybe you have a brain after all, Elaine.

ELAINE: (*Trying to sound intellectual*) I'm going to excuse that snide remark, Luke, but only because I know you're worried about your parents finding out and you're displacing your anxiety onto me.

LUKE: Huh?

BETHANY: Never mind, Luke. Her dad's a therapist.

CASEY: All right, then. It's all set.

BRIAN: Right. It will be just us. Just this group of people standing right here. No one else.

NARRATOR #1: Just then, another group of students, most of them from the girls' swim team, walks out of the mall.

BRIAN: (*Excited, but whispering*) Hey, is that Jennifer Trent?

JUSTINE: (*In a normal voice*) Who's Jennifer Trent?

BRIAN: (*Whispering again*) Shh! Keep your voice down. She'll hear you.

JUSTINE: (*Whispering, but loudly*) Who is Jennifer Trent?

BRIAN: She's sort of new. She's on the swim team. Oh no, she's coming this way. What should I say? Quick, tell me something to say to her. (*Louder now, to Jennifer*) Hey, Jennifer! How are you doing? It's me, Brian. From math class . . . I noticed you weren't in class today.

JENNIFER: We had a swim meet. I got out of 2 hours of school.

BRIAN: Wow, um, I didn't know you were on the swim team.

JENNIFER: Well, I am. It's a lot of fun.

Brian: (*Nervously*) Oh. Wow. Um . . . hey, my friend Luke is having a little get-together Saturday, in case you want to come. He has a pool, you know, at his apartment, so if you um, you know, needed to practice your backstroke or anything . . . um . . . well, you could. Practice, I mean.

JENNIFER: Okay. Maybe I'll think about it.

NARRATOR #1: To Brian's relief, Jennifer's parents pull up. She and her friends climb into the car and leave.

BRIAN: (*Embarrassed*) I can't believe how I talked to Jennifer Trent. Wow. Um. Well. Um. Uh. Wow.

JUSTINE: I, um, can't believe you invited her to the get-together.

BRIAN: (*Ignoring Justine*) How many times did I say "um"?

CASEY: Um, I, um, well, don't, um, know.

BETHANY: Um.

LUKE: Wow.

BRIAN: She and all her friends are probably all laughing at me right now. She probably thinks I'm so stupid!

BETHANY: Oh, calm down. If she does, then there's something wrong with her and you wouldn't want to go out with her anyway.

LUKE: How could you invite her to my place? We don't even know her.

BRIAN: I invited her over? Oh, I guess I did. I don't even know how it happened, Luke. I promise. I was just standing there. I didn't know what to say. That was the only thing I could think of.

TRINA: Why didn't you ask her how she did at the swim meet? Or what other teams were there?

JUSTINE: Or if she wanted to borrow your math notes?

BRIAN: Oh, *now* you tell me something to say.

LUKE: (*Shaking his head*) You invited Jennifer Trent to my place! I can't believe it!

BETHANY: Hey, Justine. There's your sister. I can't believe she's old enough to get her driver's license. She's so short!

JUSTINE: I know. Sometimes she gets pulled over just because she looks like a little kid behind the wheel. Do any of you want her to give you a ride to Luke's party Saturday?

LUKE: My *get-together*.

TRINA: I don't think I'm going. There's this movie I want to watch on TV.

KELLY: You mean you're going to miss the party of the century just to—

LUKE: It's not a party!

KELLY: You're going to miss the get-together of the century just to watch a stupid movie?

CASEY: It's probably some sappy, kissy love story, right? One of those "that's so romantic it makes you sick" movies?

ELAINE: Justine, why is your sister honking the horn so much?

JUSTINE: I don't know. Maybe she wants us to get in or something. She's so impatient.

TRINA: For your information, it's a movie about all these psycho aliens that want to completely destroy the world. Then there's this amazing woman who takes them all on.

ELAINE: And she wins.

BETHANY: Oh, great. Thanks for telling me the end.

CASEY: Hey, Luke has a big-screen TV. Why don't you just watch it over at his house?

ELAINE: The aliens will look huge!

KELLY: That honking is really annoying. Can't she see we're trying to have a conversation?

BRIAN: (*Still not paying attention to anyone else*) And then I said she could practice her backstroke in the pool at Luke's apartment. Like she would actually do that! I think I'm going to throw up.

JUSTINE: Just don't do it in my sister's car, all right? She'll never give me a ride again.

NARRATOR #2: Just then, Trina's mother pulls up behind Justine's sister.

BRIAN: Hey, Trina, your mom's pretty understanding, right? She wouldn't mind if I got sick in her car. And she likes me. Maybe I'll get a ride with you instead.

TRINA: (*Sarcastically*) Oh, great. Maybe I'll get a ride with Justine's sister then.

NARRATOR #1: The students pile into the two cars and drive off.

NARRATOR #2: Finally, the weekend comes. Luke's parents leave. Luke rides his bicycle to Brian's house, as planned.

NARRATOR #1: After spending the day together, they return to Luke's apartment. That evening, they walk to a nearby convenience store for snacks.

NARRATOR #2: While they are gone, a large crowd of students gathers in the parking lot in front of Luke's apartment building. Walking back, Brian spots the crowd first.

BRIAN: (*Nervously*) Uh, Luke, remember how we were joking about how you weren't very popular and how nobody would come to your house if you had a party?

LUKE: You guys were being pretty mean, if you ask me.

BRIAN: Well, if it's any consolation, it looks like we were also pretty wrong. Look.

NARRATOR #1: Brian points to the crowd gathered in the parking lot and waits for Luke to start yelling at him. Instead, Luke seems rather pleased.

LUKE: Whoa! Look at all those people at my place! I do know more than ten people.

BRIAN: (*Relieved that Luke isn't mad at him*) I know. I guess you're a lot more popular than any of us thought.

LUKE: Yes, you guys were all wrong. I could probably be the class president or something.

BRIAN: If all the people in your parking lot voted for you, you could.

NARRATOR #2: As the boys approach the group, Luke starts to get nervous.

LUKE: That is kind of a lot of people, huh?

BRIAN: Yes, but it probably looks like more from far away. You know how that works—things look bigger the farther away you are from them. The closer you get, the smaller they look.

LUKE: Maybe . . .

NARRATOR #2: The boys continue walking toward Luke's apartment building.

LUKE: Brian?

BRIAN: What?

LUKE: The crowd isn't looking any smaller.

BRIAN: I know. I think I might have had that whole thing backwards. Maybe things look bigger the closer you get. That makes more sense when you think about it.

LUKE: It looks like they've all got beach stuff. Who's that with the giraffe-head inner tube? And who's the person with the beach towel wrapped around his head?

BRIAN: Never mind that. Is that Kyle Graham wearing flippers and a snorkel mask? And is that a wet suit draped over his arm? He must think the pool is really deep.

NARRATOR #1: Just then, Elaine, Justine, and Kelly run up to the boys, smiling and excited.

ELAINE: Isn't this amazing? I think I underestimated how many people you know, Luke. Of course, I did help things along a little bit. I didn't want you to feel bad about being so unpopular. You can thank me later.

LUKE: What do you mean, you helped things along?

ELAINE: I used a few of my connections and spread the word about your party—all in one day! I only found out about it Thursday. Just think what I could have done if I'd known about this at the beginning of the week!

LUKE: Yes, just think.

JUSTINE: And, Luke, I knew that if you thought about it, you would want to invite Anna Conroy. I just went ahead and invited her for you.

LUKE: Who's Anna Conroy?

JUSTINE: You know, from social studies. Anyway, she brought her two cousins, who are only in town for the weekend.

LUKE: I don't even know them!

JUSTINE: Luke, I just couldn't say no to family.

BRIAN: They're not *your* family.

JUSTINE: Well, they're *someone's* family, aren't they?

KELLY: Hey, we'd better get these people into your house before the neighbors see Kyle in that ridiculous snorkel mask.

KYLE: (*Walking over to Luke and his friends*) Did I hear my name?

LUKE: Yes. Brian was saying you should take off that stupid mask. You look like that guy in those *Friday the 13th* movies.

KYLE: That guy wore a hockey mask, not a snorkel mask.

JUSTINE: (*Sarcastically*) I'm sure some guy's going to go around with a chain saw and a snorkel mask.

KELLY: Actually, it makes about as much sense as wearing a hockey mask, if you think about it.

ELAINE: And at least with a snorkel mask, he could still breathe if he ended up in a lake or something.

BRIAN: Have you guys ever noticed what stupid conversations you have? Come on, let's get everyone inside before the neighbors see.

NARRATOR #2: The students all move inside Luke's apartment. Some of them go straight out to the pool, but several stay inside to watch the alien movie Trina had mentioned at the mall. Others stand in the kitchen with Luke and watch as the apartment fills with people.

ELAINE: This is great, Luke! Can you believe all these people?

LUKE: No, I really can't.

BRIAN: What's the matter? I thought you were happy about being so popular.

LUKE: I was, but look at them. They're everywhere. And they keep coming, too.

KELLY: If you ask me, you should be proud. People are going to be talking about this for a long, long time.

LUKE: Hey, isn't that Jake Vincent over there? He cheated me out of my Skittles in first grade and now he's got the nerve to show his face at my place!

ELAINE: Don't you think you're being just a little too dramatic, Luke?

KELLY: Yes, Luke. I mean, it was just a bag of Skittles.

LUKE: He took my Snoopy thermos, too.

ELAINE: Well, while you sit here and cry over a bag of Skittles . . .

LUKE: (*Interrupting her*) And a thermos.

ELAINE: While you moan and groan about something that happened when you weren't even three feet tall, I'm going to go enjoy your party.

LUKE: (*Calling to Elaine as she walks away to the living room*) It's not a party. It's a *get-together!*

BRIAN: Come on, Luke. Why don't you go watch the movie? It sounds like one of the aliens went into a furious rage tearing apart the spaceship. That should relax you.

NARRATOR #1: Luke joins the students watching the movie. Just as Brian is about to go out to the pool, Jennifer Trent and a girl he's never seen before approach him.

BRIAN: Jennifer! Wow! I, um, uh, didn't know you were here.

JENNIFER: I just came outside. We've been watching that movie in the other room.

BRIAN: Oh. The one with the, um, UFOs.

NARRATOR #1: Before Brian can impress Jennifer any further, some of the students come in from the pool.

BRIAN: Hey, you guys, get out. You're dripping all over the floor.

CASEY: Relax, Brian. It's just water. People always put water on the floor. Haven't you ever heard of mopping?

JENNIFER: Yes, but this floor is carpeted.

CASEY: Oh, sorry. It will dry, though. Who ever heard of a kitchen floor with carpet, anyway?

BRIAN: It's always had carpet. Luke's dad likes it because he hates to mop.

KELLY: Why doesn't he just make his kids do it? That's what my parents would do.

BRIAN: (Frustrated) I don't know. Look, you're still dripping water all over the floor. You know how paranoid Luke is. If he sees this puddle, he'll panic. He'll think it will make the floor cave in or something.

NARRATOR #2: Still grumbling about the carpeting, Casey gives up and joins the others watching the movie in the living room.

NARRATOR #1: Soon after Casey sits down, tension builds in the movie.

NARRATOR #2: Just as it reaches its most suspenseful part, Kyle Graham comes in from the pool. He is dripping wet and still wearing his green flippers, a shiny black wet suit and his snorkel mask and snorkel. Seeing how involved everyone is with the film, Kyle lets out a blood curdling scream just to scare them.

NARRATOR #1: Seeing Kyle in his slippery green and black scuba gear, everyone screams. Kyle looks amazingly similar to the lead alien in the movie. Without thinking, Luke yells and grabs a pillow from the couch. Justine throws her popcorn straight into the air, and Trina jumps up from the couch, ready to run out the front door.

NARRATOR #2: When Trina jumps to her feet, she accidentally kicks Kelly's grape smoothie. Then, as if in slow motion, the drink tips over, onto the beige carpet. For a few moments, the students ignore the movie and watch as a giant, purple shape takes form on the floor.

KELLY: It looks sort of like Barney.

BETHANY : You mean the spot?

KELLY: Yes.

BETHANY: No, it doesn't.

KELLY: Yes, it does. Look. It's a side view of him.

CASEY: See the nose?

TRINA: I think it's more pointy than that.

CASEY: No. It's pretty round. They probably didn't want him to scare little kids.

BETHANY: How do you know so much about Barney?

CASEY: My little brother. He used to have Barney everything—bedspread, lunch box, you name it.

JUSTINE: Hey, I see it, too! There's an outline of him when you're looking at him from the side.

ELAINE: It *is* him! Luke, we've got Barney right here in your living room! Hey, where is Luke?

JUSTINE: He ran outside as soon as he saw the spot. Look at him now. I think he's hyperventilating. I'm going to have Brian go get him.

NARRATOR #2: Justine gets Brian, who had been in the kitchen the whole time with Jennifer, and they lead Luke back into the apartment. Luke is silent for a long time. Then he begins chattering uncontrollably. He is panicked about the large purple Barney-shaped spot on the carpet.

LUKE: Oh, my gosh! Clean it up! Get a towel. No, a rag. I don't want to stain anything else. What am I going to do? My parents are going to ground me until I'm dead. They're going to send me to military school, or worse. What if they make me go on one of those outdoor treks across the desert where they don't give you any water until you learn complete obedience, and the only thing you get to eat is canned beans?

KELLY: Gross. I hate canned food.

JUSTINE: I know. It's so disgusting. I only eat fresh vegetables.

KELLY: You know, I told my mom I wasn't eating canned or frozen vegetables anymore and that I was only eating fresh, organic stuff from now on. She said, "Fine, then you can do the cooking from now on, too." Can you believe that? I feel like saying, "Thanks for all the cancer-causing preservatives, Mom."

JUSTINE: It's that generation. They're just not *aware*, you know?

LUKE: (*Angry and panicked*) Would you guys please be quiet for one second? My life is over, and you're talking about frozen vegetables.

KELLY: It's only a stain. It's not like people brought a keg of beer in here or something. Or got drunk. Or broke furniture.

LUKE: You don't know my parents. They'll see that I lied to them. They'll never trust me again.

NARRATOR #1: Just then, the doorbell rings. Everyone stops talking and looks at Luke, who looks even more nervous than before.

LUKE: (*Still panicked*) Who could that be? Nobody else has bothered to ring the doorbell . . . or even knock. They just came on in. Oh, my gosh. I'll bet it's the police. I know it's the police. Quick, Brian, call my lawyer!

BRIAN: You don't have a lawyer.

LUKE: Oh, right . . . It's all over for me. They're going to make me sit at a table in one of those dark rooms with a light shining on me and question me until I break and tell them everything.

BETHANY: Just answer the door, Luke. The longer you wait, the worse it's going to look to whoever's out there.

NARRATOR #2: Finally, Luke answers the door with Brian at his side. It is the Warrens, the neighbors from the apartment next door.

MRS. WARREN: Luke, are you all right? What's going on over here? We heard screaming. Your parents told us you were at a friend's house. Who are all these kids? Are these all your friends?

LUKE: They're my friends . . . Well, not all of them . . . Some of them are . . .

MR. WARREN: Where are your parents? Did they come back early?

LUKE: No, they are still . . .

BRIAN: They're still at the hotel, Mr. Warren. And I'm sure they would hate to be bothered with any of this . . .

MR. WARREN: (*Loudly, to the whole room*) All right. Everybody out.

NARRATOR #1: Luke and Brian start to file out the door with the rest of the students.

MR. WARREN: Except you two.

NARRATOR #2: Lecturing them all the way, the Warrens drive Luke and Brian back to Brian's house. There the boys have to explain themselves to Brian's parents.

NARRATOR #1: Despite all of Luke's desperate hopes, the purple smoothie stain on the carpet does not magically evaporate overnight. The next day, he finds himself staring at the carpet with his parents, trying to explain the Barney-shaped spot.

LUKE: And so when Trina jumped up, she somehow kicked over the smoothie, and there you go. It's really kind of funny, Mom, if you think about it.

MRS. ANDERSON: I'm thinking about it, and it's not funny.

LUKE: Well, I mean, if you think about it for a *while*.

MRS. ANDERSON: What were you thinking, having a party when we weren't here?

LUKE: You mean you wouldn't have minded if you had been here?

MR. ANDERSON: Answer the question, Luke.

LUKE: This is worse than being questioned by the police.

MRS. ANDERSON: You were questioned by the police? Why didn't the Warrens mention that?

LUKE: No, no, no. There were no police. I was just saying—oh, never mind that. The thing is, I was keeping you from, um, dying . . . you know . . . of boredom.

MRS. ANDERSON: (*Sarcastically*) How could your having a party keep us from dying of boredom?

LUKE: Well, I can't remember. But you expected it.

MRS. ANDERSON: Expected it?

LUKE: Yes, because the kids in the movies . . .

MR. ANDERSON: Luke, enough of this. Why did you have a party?

LUKE: It wasn't a party. It was just a get-together. It was only a few people.

MR. ANDERSON: The Warrens said there were 30 kids here, at least.

LUKE: Well, you know me. I'm so bad at numbers.

MR. ANDERSON: What were you thinking?

LUKE: I was just—I don't know. I guess I was being stupid. It was a stupid thing to do. It got out of control. I'm really sorry.

MR. ANDERSON: Are you sorry you had the party or sorry you got caught?

LUKE: Well, both, I guess. I was so stressed out and worried the whole time that I couldn't really enjoy it. You can be happy about that, at least. And then the rest of the night at Brian's, all I thought about was how you both would look when you found out what happened.

MRS. ANDERSON: So what are you going to do about this stain?

NARRATOR #1: Luke has no answer to the question, but his parents do. At school Monday morning, he tells his friends at lunch.

LUKE: They're making me pay for a "professional" to come in and clean up the stain. And not just the stain—the whole carpet. I have to pay for the whole living room carpet to be cleaned. And those guys aren't cheap, either. In fact, I think I may become a carpet cleaner when I'm older. They make a lot of money.

BRIAN: So are you going with us to the mall after school?

LUKE: Are you kidding? I'm grounded for 3 weeks. You mean you're *not*? The Warrens told your parents everything they told mine.

KELLY: Hey, did you know your mom called my parents and told them about the party? It turns out she knows them from some club they're all in or something. From now on, we should do everything we can to keep our parents from knowing each other. Anyway, it's not like I had anything to do with that get-together.

ELAINE: My parents were mad, but all they did was give me a lecture. You know, "We trusted you, and look what you did. We're so disappointed . . . "

LUKE: But they didn't ground you or anything?

ELAINE: No. My dad said my guilty conscience was enough punishment.

LUKE: What about you, Brian?

BRIAN: Just the lecture—which was horrible, believe me. I mostly just sat there and nodded.

LUKE: I can't believe this. I have to pay for a whole carpet to be cleaned, and I get grounded for 3 weeks. All you have to do is sit and nod for 10 minutes.

BRIAN: Hey, that lecture lasted at least half an hour. I missed most of *Buffy the Vampire Slayer*, and sitting and nodding is a lot harder than you would think.

ELAINE: Look at it this way, Luke. Yes, you got grounded for 3 weeks, but you also got all the glory, too.

LUKE: Glory? What are you talking about? Everyone is going to remember me as the guy whose neighbors busted his party.

ELAINE: No, people will be talking about how great it was . . .

LUKE: You think so?

ELAINE: . . . well, at least it was for a little while . . . Then it was terrible . . .

BRIAN: Oh, by the way. Did you guys hear about the baseball game next weekend? It's all anyone can talk about. Maybe a few of us could have a little get-together . . .

NARRATOR #1: Luke throws a bag of potato chips at Brian. Brian smiles.

BRIAN: Or maybe *not* . . .

To Talk About

1. Does Luke really want his friends to persuade him to have a party? How do you know?

2. What arguments do Luke's friends use to persuade him to have a party? Which arguments hold the most weight with him?

3. Do you think Luke had a good time at the party? How do you know?

4. Luke agrees that only eight people will be invited to the party. However, 30 people show up. How does that happen?

5. The only damage done to Luke's apartment is a purple stain on the carpet. Do you think there would probably be more or less damage to the apartment in real life? Why?

6. What kind of relationship does Luke have with his parents? How can you tell from the play?

7. In the end, what does Luke gain by having the party? What does he lose?

8. Do you think that Luke is relieved at all when the Warrens break up the party? Why or why not?

To Write About

1. Luke lets himself be talked into having the party. Have you ever let yourself be talked into something you wanted to do but knew you shouldn't? Explain.

2. Who has more influence over you, your parents or your friends? Explain.

3. Often, friends can be a very good influence on each other. Think about a time when a friend of yours influenced you in a good way. Describe what happened.

4. Is Luke's punishment a fair one? Why or why not?

5. Do Brian and Elaine's parents treat them fairly? Why or why not?

6. Who is most to blame for the party—Luke, Brian, Elaine, or someone else? Explain.

7. Is grounding a fair punishment for people your age? Why or why not?

8. Do you think young people really believe they can have a "secret" party and not get caught? Why or why not?

9. In the play, Brian and Luke's parents don't check with each other about the overnight plans. Do you think that is realistic? Why or why not?

10. If you had to change one thing in the play that would, in your experience, make it seem more true-to-life, what would it be? Explain.

Euphemisms

When the students in the play call the party a "get-together," they are using what's called a *euphemism*. A euphemism is a milder term that is substituted for a more direct, harsh, or offensive word. For example, in the sentence, "This apartment is quite cozy," *cozy* could be a euphemism for *tiny and cramped*. When people talk of death, they sometimes say *passed away*, which is a euphemism for *died*.

People use euphemisms to soften reality or to make things sound less harsh or distasteful than they really are. Sometimes euphemisms are used out of kindness. Sometimes they are used to hide or obscure the truth. For example, describing a friend's dog as *a little slow in catching on* instead of *dumb* could be intended as a kindness. But describing a dog for sale as *skittish around strangers* might be hiding the fact that the dog is really *vicious*.

Here are some euphemistic statements a teacher might use to describe a student, if the teacher wanted to be kind. How might the teacher reword each statement if he or she wanted to be more blunt?

1. Hannah doesn't always rely on her own work. _____

2. Joshua just loves interacting with others. _____

3. Katy has a lot of confidence in her leadership ability. _____

4. Andrew has some trouble focusing his energy. _____

5. Wendy is so independent. _____

Now write three sentences of your own that use euphemisms. After each sentence, write another version of the sentence that does *not* use a euphemism.

Example: *I'm not really that fond of asparagus. (Asparagus makes me throw up.)*

_____

_____

_____

_____

_____

_____

A Good Argument?

Luke's friends make several arguments that persuade him to have the party even though he knows he shouldn't. Some of the arguments seem to make sense until they are examined further. Then they seem ridiculous. It seems people can make what appears to be a good argument for just about anything. Take a look at the five statements below. Write a good (but "pretend") argument supporting at least three of the following statements.

- Children under 5 should eat only chocolate for breakfast.
- Everyone should own a ferret.
- Everyone should have to ride the bus.
- Only boys should have to take out the trash.
- All teenagers should get big allowances.

Example:

    Statement: *Children under 5 should eat only chocolate for breakfast.*

    Argument: *Children under 5 should eat only chocolate for breakfast because parents would have an easy time fixing breakfast in the morning. All they would have to do is open a candy bar.*

Statement: _____

Argument: _____

_____

Statement: _____

Argument: _____

_____

Statement: _____

Argument: _____

_____

Statement: _____

Argument: _____

_____

It's Not a Party—It's a Get-Together!

That Only Happens in the Movies

In the play, Justine explains to her friends that Luke's parents won't find out about the party because "that only happens in the movies." There are a lot of things that only happen in the movies. If someone is carrying groceries, there is always a baguette poking out of the brown paper bag. (It seems that plastic bags are never used in the movies.) When someone comes into a house and leaves the door open, you can be sure that something awful or embarrassing is going to come in that door soon. If someone dies, it's never the main character.

Some of these things, of course, happen occasionally in real life, but not most of the time. With your group, think of five more things that always happen in the movies, but not always in real life. Then explain what would be more realistic.

Example: Movies: *When corporations try to buy out the "little guy," a group of friends come up with some creative way to raise enough money to win against the corporation.*

Real life: *Corporations buy out people every day with no struggles.*

1. Movies: _____

   Real life: _____

2. Movies: _____

   Real life: _____

3. Movies: _____

   Real life: _____

4. Movies: _____

   Real life: _____

5. Movies: _____

   Real life: _____

Now, look over your list. Would it be a good idea for movies to portray life more realistically? Why or why not? Would they be more interesting? Would they be more boring?

Romeo, Romeo! Wherefore Art Thy Costume?

CHARACTERS

Narrator #1
Narrator #2
Mr. Slade
Coach Hart
Ms. Norman

Students (male):
    Rob (playing Romeo)
    Tyson
    Bernie
    Mike
    Chris
    Jordan

Students (female):
    Jessica (playing Juliet)
    Angie
    Haley
    Gina
    Kelly
    Tara

NARRATOR #1: The cast of the spring play, *Romeo and Juliet*, is rehearsing in the school auditorium.

ROB: (*Playing Romeo*) Farewell, farewell! One kiss, and I'll descend.

JESSICA: (*Playing Juliet*) Art thou gone so? Love. . . . (*Cutting him short*) Wait! Cut! It's no use, Mr. Slade. I just can't get into my part without my costume. Mr. Slade . . . Mr. Slade?

MR. SLADE: (*Startled*) Oh! Excuse me. What did you say, Jessica? I must have been daydreaming.

TYSON: (*Under his breath to himself*) So what else is new?

JESSICA: What I was saying, Mr. Slade, is how am I supposed to feel Juliet's agony and pain when I'm wearing jeans and a T-shirt? This is never going to work.

ROB: I agree, Mr. Slade. It's hard enough pretending to like Jessica . . .

JESSICA: (*Interrupting him*) Rob, when we're in rehearsal you're supposed to call me "Juliet," remember? We've only been doing this for 2 whole months.

ROB: As I was saying, before Juliet here opened her big mouth and interrupted me, how can I even pretend to fall in love with someone who's wearing a T-shirt with the Spitting Leos on it? I know I'm a good actor and all, but isn't that going a little too far? I mean, who likes that band?

JESSICA: I happen to like the Spitting Leos quite a lot. If nobody likes them, why is their concert sold out? Tell me that. And while you're at it, how about telling me how I'm supposed to fall hopelessly in love with a Romeo who has purple hair?

MR. SLADE: She does, uh, have a point there, Rob—I mean Romeo. The costumes aren't going to look right if you insist on keeping your hair purple.

TARA: Don't listen to Jessica, Mr. Slade. Rob's—I mean, Romeo's—hair color is the only cool thing about him.

ROB: Thanks, Tara—I think.

TYSON: All I have to say is that when I get my hands on the person who stole those costumes, he'd better watch out.

JESSICA: What do you mean he? Everybody knows it was Crystal Thompson who stole those costumes.

ROB: Oh, come on. You're just jealous because Steven Burns asked her and not you to go to the concert with him. The whole school knows you like him.

JESSICA: I do not like him! What would anyone see in Steven Burns, anyway? You're just mad because I told Bethany what a terrible skier you are.

ROB: (*Surprised*) You told Bethany I was a terrible skier? How could you do that?

JESSICA: It was easy. I just opened my mouth . . .

ROB: You mean your big mouth . . .

MR. SLADE: Rob and Jessica, stop arguing right now before I throw both of you out of this play! The costumes have not been stolen. They've just been . . . misplaced. I'm sure that's all it is. You know, once I misplaced my car. It was a 1991 Mazda. Bright red, too. I rode my bike around for a week before I finally remembered where I'd parked it . . . Now that was a good little car, not like the one I've got now. All the doors stick and the transmission needs work. Sometimes the brakes don't quite work either . . . Well, in any case, I'm just saying that things can get lost. I misplace my billfold all the time . . . and my keys. I'm sure the same thing has happened to those costumes. They have just been misplaced. The principal is working as hard as he can to track them down. I'm certain we will have them in our hands long before opening night.

TARA: Mr. Slade, it's only one week before opening night. This was supposed to be a dress rehearsal, remember? Opening night is next Friday.

MR. SLADE: (*Surprised*) Oh! Yes, I guess you're right. Time really flies, doesn't it? It seems like just yesterday that I, I mean we, had 2 long and painfully grueling months of rehearsal ahead of us. Well, I'm sure Principal Wiggins will find the costumes soon. I'm sure he knows just where to look for them.

JESSICA: I hope he looks in Crystal Thompson's locker.

MR. SLADE: I don't want to hear any rumors flying around about who stole those costumes. So far, only the drama department and Principal Wiggins know they are missing. Let's keep it that way. If you have any suspicions, keep them to yourselves. Now, let's get back to work.

NARRATOR #1: Reluctantly, the cast members take their places and resume the rehearsal.

NARRATOR #2: The following Monday, Haley, the editor of the school newspaper, talks to some friends during P.E. class. They discuss the missing costumes while they do their warm-ups.

ANGIE: Everybody says it was Crystal Thompson. She's the one who stole the costumes.

HALEY: But why would she do that? What would anyone want with a bunch of clothes made for the 16th century? I mean, it's not like those clothes are coming back into style or anything.

GINA: Can you picture it? Darren Perkins in tights and knickers!

ANGIE: Actually, everyone's saying Crystal was just jealous because she didn't get a part in the play. That's a pretty good reason to steal the costumes, don't you think?

GINA: Sure. I can't think of a better way to ruin a play than to make everyone go without costumes.

HALEY: And Crystal is just the kind of person to do something sneaky like that. Remember that time she dunked my new jacket right in the swimming pool, just because she was mad about . . . well, I don't remember what she was mad about. I just remember she took the jacket out of my gym locker and dropped it in the pool.

GINA: Did you ever get the chlorine smell out? I'd like to borrow it if you did.

HALEY: Nope. You're out of luck. My mom even took it to the dry cleaner, but it still reeks.

COACH HART: Gessler, you're doing about half as many sit-ups as the rest of the class. Pick up the pace.

ANGIE: Okay, Mr. Hart.

GINA: So you still have that jacket even though it smells like a swimming pool?

HALEY: Yes. I spent a whole month's allowance on it. I can't bring myself to throw it away.

COACH HART: Gessler, pick up your feet. They're called jumping jacks for a reason, you know.

ANGIE: I wish he would stop calling me "Gessler" all the time. Doesn't he know my first name by now? I mean, he's only been jogging with my dad every evening for 2 years, and . . .

GINA: Let's get back to Crystal.

ANGIE: Oh, yes. The whole reason I'm telling you all this is because I think it would be a good story for the paper.

HALEY: Are you kidding? We don't have any hard facts. We can't just print some rumor in the paper without any proof.

ANGIE: We know the costumes are missing, don't we? And we know Crystal was mad about not getting a part in the play, right? What more do you need?

HALEY: We need more than that. Lots of people didn't get a part in the play.

GINA: Yes, but no one else was as mad about it as Crystal.

ANGIE: She's right. Everyone said Crystal was furious.

HALEY: Who is everyone, anyway?

ANGIE: Well, I don't know. All I'm saying is that this would make a good story for the newspaper. You haven't forgotten about the state journalism competition, have you?

GINA: That's right. A story like this might have a chance of winning, and you would have the satisfaction of getting back at Crystal for ruining that cool jacket I wanted to borrow.

ANGIE: It would be great to run a fast-breaking story like this on the front page.

HALEY: It would be better than what we've got lined up right now. That's for sure.

ANGIE: What do we have right now?

HALEY: (*Sighing*) Nothing. Nothing at all.

COACH HART: Everyone! Five laps around the field. Now!

NARRATOR #1: That afternoon, Haley and the rest of the reporters for the *Morrissey School Tribune* meet in the cafeteria to think of stories for the next issue.

BERNIE: I know! What if I do a photo feature on all the latest in body piercing?

JORDAN: We already did a story on that.

BERNIE: We did?

JORDAN: Yes. I guess it was before you joined the newspaper staff. We got a lot of letters on the subject, mostly from parents calling piercing "body mutilation."

KELLY: And some others from kids saying that piercing is a kind of art.

MIKE: If it's art, then why doesn't the Mona Lisa have a nose ring?

BERNIE: Maybe she does and her parents just painted over it.

HALEY: Before this gets any more stupid, let me say that what I'd really like for this issue is something serious. This is the issue we're entering in the state journalism competition, you know.

JORDAN: Well, what do you want, Haley? I mean, it's not like anything that important ever happens around here.

KELLY: The school play opens this weekend. That's kind of important, at least for people in this school.

JORDAN: But we'll be competing with newspapers from schools all over the state, schools that have exciting things happen all the time.

BERNIE: (*Excitedly*) Yes, stuff like fights and vandalism and protests and crimes!

NARRATOR #2: Just then Ms. Norman, the school nurse, approaches the group of students.

MS. NORMAN: Hello, kids. Let's see . . . Jordan, Kelly, Mike, Haley. Must be a newspaper meeting.

BERNIE: (*Jokingly*) Actually, it's a meeting of the school's most dangerous rebel forces. I am the fearless leader.

MS. NORMAN: Oh, is it? Well, did the "fearless leader" get that splinter out of his finger all right? I know he was a little worried it would have to be amputated when he came to my office yesterday.

BERNIE: (*Embarrassed*) Yes, I got it out fine . . . Do you have a bandage, though? I bumped it on my desk this morning, and the pain shot up my arm like a missile.

MS. NORMAN: I think I could rummage up a bandage if I looked hard enough.

NARRATOR #1: Ms. Norman talks with the students a bit longer and then goes back to her office.

HALEY: Did you know Ms. Norman was named School Nurse of the Year?

ANGIE: I didn't even know there was such a thing.

JORDAN: What do you have to do to get that? Change a bed pan in 20 seconds or less?

KELLY: You are so disgusting.

MIKE: She doesn't change bed pans. She wraps sprained ankles and takes your temperature—stuff like that.

BERNIE: And removes splinters.

GINA: Can we get back to the subject, please? I know how we can win the contest.

HALEY: How?

GINA: Print the story on Crystal Thompson stealing those costumes. I've already written it.

HALEY: I told you—we don't have any proof. It wouldn't be right to say something so bad about her without even knowing if it's true.

ANGIE: You didn't mind saying bad things about her after she ruined your jacket.

HALEY: It wasn't like I told the whole school about it. I just told you guys and a few other people.

BERNIE: You told our whole homeroom.

MIKE: And our whole social studies class.

KELLY: And everybody at Jade Matthews' birthday party.

HALEY: Not everybody at Jade's party.

KELLY: Only the 20 or so people on the back porch.

HALEY: Well, you're forgetting an important part of this. Five people, including the custodian, saw her dump it in the swimming pool. There were witnesses.

ANGIE: Everybody started locking up their jackets during gym after that, so our clothes would be safe.

JORDAN: See, telling was all for the best.

BERNIE: Not for Crystal. Nobody talked to her for a whole week after that.

HALEY: It could have been even worse for her. What if what she did had been printed up somewhere?

KELLY: Writing something makes it more official or something.

MIKE: So what if it's official? The way I see it, if she took your jacket, then what would keep her from taking those costumes?

KELLY: Maybe Haley has a point. If we knew for sure Crystal took those costumes, and she admitted it, then it might be different. But we don't, and she won't, so it isn't. Does that make sense?

ALL: No.

KELLY: But you know what I mean, right?

ALL: No.

KELLY: I just mean that if we print that story, everyone will believe it. People believe anything once it's written down. (*Dramatically*) She'll live out her days in complete isolation. No one will want to talk to her. No one will sit by her at lunch. No one will ask her to any dances. No one will go with her to Spring Fest.

MIKE: What Spring Fest? We don't have any Spring Fest.

KELLY: I guess that's true. I must have seen a Spring Fest on some TV show. Still, no one will want anything to do with Crystal, and that would be horrible—especially if she didn't take the costumes.

GINA: What do you mean "if she didn't take the costumes"? Of course she took the costumes!

HALEY: What proof do you have?

GINA: Greg Sanders said he saw her hanging around the auditorium the other day after school.

KELLY: Maybe she was waiting for someone.

CHRIS: Janet saw her rip the list of cast members off the wall when she found out she didn't get a part in the play.

KELLY: That doesn't make her a thief. It just makes her a sore loser.

ANGIE: And Gwen Tyler saw her walking around in a plumed hat and knickers.

HALEY: Really?

ANGIE: Just kidding . . . But practically the whole school knows she took those costumes. Everyone except you, that is.

CHRIS: So what are we going to do, Haley? Are we going to run the story on Crystal or not?

HALEY: I don't know.

JORDAN: All I know is I'm definitely going to be at that play on opening night when Jessica Peters has to play Juliet without the right costume. Can you believe how furious she's going to be? She's such a prima donna!

CHRIS: Jordan, do you just hang out with your dictionary all day or what? You're always throwing around words like *prima donna*.

KELLY: So what is a prima donna, anyway?

JORDAN: It's someone who thinks she's really great and should get all the attention. Oh, and just so you know, I don't hang out with my dictionary. Prima donna was today's word on my Word-a-Day calendar. You should get one, Chris.

CHRIS: But if I did, then I'd be as annoying as you.

NARRATOR #1: Wednesday evening during rehearsal, the tension is high. The costumes have still not been found, and everyone is nervous.

JESSICA: Wait! Hold it! Mr. Slade, Rob is deliberately trying to make me forget my lines.

ROB: No, I'm not. I'm just standing here.

JESSICA: He's sending subliminal messages, Mr. Slade. And, being the sensitive person that I am, I pick up on every single one of his rude, unspoken messages.

ROB: She's crazy, Mr. Slade. I'm not playing any mind games with her.

NARRATOR #2: The students continue arguing, but Mr. Slade isn't listening. He's busy coughing and sneezing from all the dust he was exposed to in the school's basement, where he was looking for the costumes.

MR. SLADE: Tyson, run out to my car and grab the box of tissues off the front seat. I can't take this scratchy bargain tissue the school buys any longer.

NARRATOR #1: Pleased to leave the tense auditorium, Tyson drags Tara with him and runs out to Mr. Slade's car.

TARA: It feels good to get out of there for a minute.

TYSON: Yes. If you ask me, Jessica and Rob should have both been kicked out a long time ago. Hey, there's no tissue in here . . . Mr. Slade is so weird.

TARA: Check in the back seat. Or maybe the trunk.

TYSON: (*Clicking the trunk lever and going to look inside*) Look at this.

TARA: It's the costumes!

NARRATOR #2: Tyson and Tara carry the missing costumes into the auditorium. Mr. Slade is happy to see them. As soon as he sees them, he remembers where he had put them.

NARRATOR #1: Finally, the opening night of the play rolls around. When the curtain goes up, the actors are all in full costume, right down to their knickers and tights.

NARRATOR #2: After the performance, Haley and some of the other students discuss the performance.

JORDAN: So, what happened? Did Jessica's fairy godmother rush in with the costumes at the last minute, or what?

CHRIS: Maybe Crystal returned them right before the show.

BERNIE: Or maybe she got caught. Maybe someone raided her house and found them.

JORDAN: I'll bet it was Jessica. She probably broke into Crystal's house and took the costumes back when no one was home.

HALEY: Before you guys decide that every girl in this school is a thief, you might want to know that Crystal didn't have the costumes at all.

ANGIE: She didn't?

CHRIS: She didn't?

JORDAN: She didn't?

HALEY: (*To each one*) No. No. And no.

ANGIE: Well, then what happened to them? Where were they all that time?

HALEY: It turns out they were in the trunk of a car.

KELLY: You mean the costumes for the play were kidnapped?

ANGIE: Why would Crystal put the costumes in the trunk of a car? She doesn't even have a car.

HALEY: I told you, Crystal didn't do anything with the costumes. And why would you say they were kidnapped?

KELLY: Well, it just seems like whenever someone's kidnapped, that's where they always find the person—in the trunk of a car.

HALEY: You are so weird. Anyway, they were in the trunk of Mr. Slade's car.

MIKE: Mr. Slade stole the costumes to his own play? Wow! A teacher stole something! We have to run this story right away.

HALEY: Stop and listen! Mr. Slade put them in there to take them to be dry cleaned. Then he forgot about them. The costumes have been in his car all along.

MIKE: There goes our great story.

HALEY: You know Mr. Slade. He is so absentminded. If you ever take a class from him, make a copy of all your homework before you turn it in.

BERNIE: No kidding. I've loaned him about a thousand pencils, and he's lost every single one.

HALEY: Anyway, the costumes never even made it to the dry cleaner.

GINA: Is that why there was a big blue splotch on Jessica's costume?

HALEY: Yes. It was left over from some past performance. I guess she was pretty mad about it. And Rob made fun of her for it right before the first act.

KELLY: So that's why she was clenching her fists the whole time. And that's why Rob looked so scared when he had to kiss her.

BERNIE: That makes a lot more sense. I kept thinking it was the lighting, but that must have been real fear on Rob's face.

MIKE: Jessica might be a prima donna, but she's also a kick boxer. I did a story on her once for the newspaper.

GINA: So what are we going to do for a story now?

MIKE: How about doing it on how Ms. Norman is the School Nurse of the Year?

ANGIE: School Nurse of the Year? That's the most boring thing I've ever heard.

HALEY: At least it doesn't involve libel.

ANGIE: What's libel?

JORDAN: I can't believe you work on the school newspaper and you don't know what libel is.

ANGIE: So what is it?

JORDAN: Well, it's, you know . . . It's difficult to explain . . . It . . .

GINA: It obviously hasn't been Word of the Day yet on Jordan's calendar . . . Don't worry, Jordan. I'm sure it will come up in the next month or so.

HALEY: Libel is when you publish something that isn't true about someone and what you publish makes someone look bad.

BERNIE: Yes, but if you don't know it's not true, then how can it be libel?

HALEY: Because if you print something, you're supposed to know it is true or at least be able to give some evidence that it *might* be true. Otherwise, we could print a story that said two aliens landed their spaceship on Oak Street last night. We don't know it isn't true, but we don't have any reason to believe it is, either.

BERNIE: Whenever I imagine aliens coming to Earth, I don't picture them landing here, in this town. Even aliens know that nothing exciting ever happens here.

JORDAN: It would be exciting if we all got sued for libel.

HALEY: Yes, it would probably be exciting—not exactly pleasant, but exciting.

JORDAN: And it would make a great story for the newspaper.

HALEY: Yes, I can see it now: "Newspaper staff gets sued for libel."

JORDAN: Well, maybe not *that* good a story . . .

To Talk About

1. What makes the students think Crystal stole the costumes? What "evidence" do the students have?

2. From reading the play, what do you know about Crystal? What kind of person is she? How do you know?

3. What clues can you find in the play that Mr. Slade may be responsible for the missing costumes?

4. Based on the play, what are three reasons Haley might want to print the story about Crystal stealing the costumes?

5. Based on the play, what are three reasons Haley might *not* want to print the story about Crystal stealing the costumes?

To Write About

1. Crystal is apparently very disappointed at not getting a role in *Romeo and Juliet*. Think about a time in your own life when you were disappointed with yourself. What caused your disappointment? How did you handle it? Write about your experience with disappointment.

2. Crystal has no lines in the play. Give her a voice by writing her into a scene. What kind of personality do you think she should have? What would she have to say about not getting a role in *Romeo and Juliet*?

3. Imagine a different ending for the play. Write your own version, starting soon after Ms. Norman appears.

4. Have you ever been accused of doing something you didn't do? Tell what happened. How did you feel? What did you do?

Responsibilities

In the play, Haley, the editor of the school newspaper, is tempted to publish a story accusing someone she dislikes of stealing. In the end, though, she realizes her job at the newspaper is more than just writing stories. Part of her job is making sure that what goes into the paper is true.

Like editing a newspaper, many jobs involve more responsibility than just the obvious. For example, a tree surgeon's obvious responsibility is to cut branches off trees, but he or she has other responsibilities as well: making sure the falling branches don't hurt a passerby and making sure not to cut off so many limbs that the tree dies.

For each of the jobs listed below, write down the obvious responsibilities of the person performing the job, and then write down the not so obvious, but just as important, responsibilities.

Cab driver

Obvious responsibilities   Not so obvious responsibilities

_____   _____

_____   _____

_____   _____

_____   _____

Dog walker

Obvious responsibilities   Not so obvious responsibilities

_____   _____

_____   _____

_____   _____

_____   _____

Teacher

Obvious responsibilities   Not so obvious responsibilities

_____   _____

_____   _____

_____   _____

_____   _____

Babysitter

Obvious responsibilities   Not so obvious responsibilities

_____   _____

_____   _____

_____   _____

_____   _____

House painter

Obvious responsibilities   Not so obvious responsibilities

_____   _____

_____   _____

_____   _____

_____   _____

Chef

Obvious responsibilities   Not so obvious responsibilities

_____   _____

_____   _____

_____   _____

_____   _____

That's What You Think

Some of the students in "Romeo, Romeo!" draw false conclusions. For example, they see Crystal Thompson react very angrily to the news that she has not been cast in the school play. They conclude that she has stolen the costumes. However, she does not, in fact, have anything at all to do with the disappearance of the costumes.

It is natural and usually very reasonable to draw conclusions based on what we have seen. However, it is important to understand that the obvious conclusion may not always be the correct conclusion. If we are not careful, we can end up believing things that are completely untrue.

Take a look at the two situations described below. With each situation, it is easy to draw a quick and obvious conclusion about what happened, based on the facts given. However, imagine that things aren't that simple. For each situation, come up with a not-so-obvious explanation for what happened.

1. You walk into the kitchen where the beautiful chocolate cake you baked for your friend's birthday party is sitting. Unfortunately, half the cake is missing. Then your younger brother walks into the room with crumbs on his shirt and a dab of frosting on his cheek. Knowing your little brother, you assume he ate half the cake. What *really* happened? _____

_____

_____

2. Your somewhat reckless friend Carlos loves to race dirt bikes, especially because he thinks it impresses girls. In fact, the more girls who are watching, the more reckless he becomes. He loves to take the corners really fast and make his bike jump off the hills. One weekend Carlos enters a big bike race, and a girl he really likes is rumored to be watching the event. The following Monday, Carlos shows up at school with a broken toe. What *really* happened? _____

_____

_____

Now write a short paragraph describing a time when you drew a wrong conclusion. Give the facts pointing to an obvious conclusion. Then describe what *really* happened. (If you cannot think of such a time, describe an imaginary situation.)

_____

_____

_____

_____

Urban Legends

In "Romeo, Romeo," the rumor about Crystal Thompson is circulated as if it is the truth. Of course, it is not the truth at all.

Another kind of untruth that circulates all the time is the urban legend. Through forwarded e-mail messages, gossip, and just sharing what others have told us happened "to someone my aunt knows" or "someone my dad's boss knows," these legends are passed on as if they are fact. In fact, they almost always are *not* true. Here are just a few urban legends:

- Did you ever hear about the guy who had his kidney stolen while on vacation in Las Vegas? One night someone knocked him out in his hotel room, removed one of his kidneys and left him with a chunk of ice packed over the incision. (There is absolutely no evidence that this ever happened to anyone.)
- Did you hear about the 7-year-old boy dying of cancer, who just wants to get into the *Guiness Book of World Records* before he dies? He wants people to send him their business cards, so that he can collect more than anyone in the world. (The boy is now 19 years old, long cured of cancer, and sick of getting business cards in the mail.)
- Did you hear about the famous store-restaurant that had wonderful chocolate chip cookies? It seems that a customer liked the cookies so much that she asked for the recipe. The waiter said he could give it to her only if he charged her "two fifty." She agreed, and was later shocked to find a "$250.00" charge on her credit card, instead of $2.50. When she complained, the store refused to remove the charge, saying that it wasn't his fault she misunderstood "two fifty" to mean two dollars and fifty cents. The customer decided to get revenge by forwarding the recipe by e-mail to everyone she knew and asking them to forward the recipe to as many people as possible. (Not true. The story features different well-known stores, depending upon which version is forwarded. No one has ever been able to find any evidence that any of the many versions of this story are true. However, it *is* a good story.)
- Did you hear about the danger of making a deposit at an automatic teller machine? A customer died licking a deposit envelope at a teller machine in Toronto. It seemed the glue on the envelope was laced with cyanide. An inspection of other envelopes from teller machines in the area revealed more poisoned envelopes. (Not true. The Department of Public Health in Toronto has no record of such a poisoning, or of finding poisoned envelopes.)

What features of the stories above make them believable? What human worries and fears does each address? What urban legends have you heard? You might even wish to do some research on the Internet or consult some of the books on the subject. Some interesting references are:

The Best Book of Urban Myths Ever! by Yorick Brown and Mike Flynn, Carlton Books
The Choking Doberman: And Other Urban Legends, by Jan Harold Brunvand, W. W. Norton
The Vanishing Hitchhiker: American Urban Legends and Their Meanings, by Jan Harold Brunvand, W. W. Norton
Urban Legends: The As-Complete-As-One-Could-Be Guide to Modern Myths by N. E. Genge, Three Rivers Press
Urban Legends: The Truth Behind All Those Deliciously Entertaining Myths That Are Absolutely, Positively, 100% Not True, by Richard Roeper, New Page Books

Foreshadowing

At the beginning of the play "Romeo, Romeo," there are a few indications that Mr. Slade, the director, has something to do with the missing costumes. One hint is that he doesn't even realize his own production is opening in one week. Furthermore, he admits that he loses everything, even his Mazda. These hints show us that he is clearly absentminded.

The costumes are finally found in the trunk of Mr. Slade's car. Without actually coming right out and telling us, the writer has set up the conclusion of the story from the very beginning, using *foreshadowing*. Foreshadowing involves presenting an indication or suggestion of what is to follow in a story.

Foreshadowing helps make the conclusion of a story believable. What if the writer hadn't mentioned how forgetful Mr. Slade is? To have his forgetfulness pop out of nowhere at the end of the play would not have been believable, and the reader would have felt cheated. It is for this reason that foreshadowing is especially important in mystery writing.

Imagine that you are a famous mystery writer. Your new short story, "The Case of the Missing Bedroom Slippers" tells about the disappearance of Jill Prell's favorite bedroom slippers. At the end of the story, Jill sees hundreds of tiny ants crawling into her closet, all heading toward one spot. Suddenly, she knows it is her sister who stole the bedroom slippers.

What foreshadowing could help make your story believable? Below is one example. Write three more.

Example:

> Evidence against Jill's sister: *The ants are heading toward a large drip of butter pecan ice cream.*
> Foreshadowing: *Earlier in the story, someone mentions that Jill's sister works at Baskin-Robbins.*

1. Evidence against Jill's sister:_____

    _____

    _____

2. Evidence against Jill's sister:_____

    _____

    _____

3. Evidence against Jill's sister:_____

    _____

    _____

Promise You Won't Get Mad

CHARACTERS

Narrator #1
Narrator #2
Mr. Johnson
Mrs. Johnson

Students (male):
Greg
Vincent
Bernie
Karl
Jacob

Students (female):
Alicia
Elizabeth
Janet
Robyn
Bethany

NARRATOR #1: At the mall, Alicia is admiring a sweater she wants but can't afford. Alicia's friends are getting tired of hearing her talk about it.

ELIZABETH: Can't we go get some caramel corn now? Standing here staring at this sweater isn't going to make it any cheaper.

JANET: Besides, I need to get out of here pretty soon and get ready for hockey.

ALICIA: What do you have to do to get ready for hockey? Hit yourself in the mouth with your stick a few times?

JANET: (*Annoyed*) Actually, I have to put on about 15 pounds of padding and then get into the rink and stretch and warm up.

ALICIA: Sorry. I'm just mad because I don't have the money for this sweater.

ROBYN: I don't see why you care so much about it. I mean, it's nice and everything, but it's just a sweater.

ALICIA: It's not just *a* sweater. It's *the* sweater. I want to wear it to the basketball game next Friday.

JANET: People are going to be watching the game, not you.

BETHANY: If you really want it, why don't you just get a job and use your first check to buy it?

ROBYN: (*Sarcastically*) Who's going to hire someone who isn't even old enough to drive?

ALICIA: The only thing people our age are allowed to do is babysit. I'd have to watch the Marshak kids for about 15 years to pay for that sweater.

ROBYN: They would be in college by the time you earned the money.

ALICIA: And by that time, the sweater would be out of style.

ELIZABETH: And the basketball game would be over.

JANET: Maybe that should tell you something. Maybe it would be stupid to buy this sweater even if you *did* have the money. Come on, let's go.

ALICIA: (*Kidding around as she fantasizes*) Maybe if I stand here long enough, the store manager will come by and see how much I want it and sell it to me for less. Maybe he'll see how beautiful I would look in it. Maybe . . .

BETHANY: Maybe he'll think you're scoping out the place and waiting for a chance to steal the sweater.

ALICIA: Very funny.

ROBYN: It's true. Store employees always act like kids our age are going to steal something.

ELIZABETH: I know. It's just a stupid stereotype.

ALICIA: What's a stupid stereotype?

ELIZABETH: The idea that teenagers can't be trusted.

ROBYN: When you're little, everyone thinks you're really cute and cuddly and you can't do anything wrong. Then the second you turn 13, people act like you're a villain or something.

ALICIA: I'm the same sweet person I always was—except I'm much taller and more beautiful.

BETHANY: Sweet?

ELIZABETH: Beautiful?

ALICIA: Yes. People get much better looking around this age.

ELIZABETH: You're 2½ months older than me!

ALICIA: I guess that means you won't be beautiful for another 2½ months.

JANET: (*Changing the subject*) Look who is walking straight toward us.

ROBYN: Who?

BETHANY: Greg Sanders.

ALICIA: Greg Sanders? He's coming toward us right now? Oh, my gosh, do I look all right?

BETHANY: Yes, except your bottom lip is sticking out about a mile from pouting over that sweater.

NARRATOR #2: Just then, Greg and his friends Karl, Vincent, and Bernie approach the four girls.

GREG: Hey there, Bethany. Where have you been all my life?

BETHANY: Standing here looking at this sweater Alicia wants. And by the way, Greg, you need to get a new pick-up line. You sound like a soap opera.

GREG: (*Ignoring her*) Why are you standing here staring at the sweater? Why don't you just go buy it?

VINCENT: Because they're girls, that's why. Girls always take forever to buy clothes.

BETHANY: See, Alicia—another stereotype.

GREG: No, really. Why don't you just go buy it if you want it so bad? You're practically drooling all over it anyway.

ELIZABETH: First, she does not drool. Second, it's none of your business why she's not buying it.

GREG: It is if I make it my business.

ROBYN: Bethany's right, Greg. You do sound like a soap opera. All you need is for some music to play every time you say something.

JANET: (*Impatient to end the conversation and go to hockey practice*) The reason she's not buying it is because it's too expensive, all right?

BERNIE: Too expensive? You should have said something earlier.

ALICIA: What do you mean?

BERNIE: Greg here has the perfect solution to all your money troubles.

GREG: Bernie, don't show them . . .

VINCENT: (*Ignoring him*) Look what we have.

NARRATOR #1: Despite Greg's attempts to stop them, the boys pull several metal slugs out of their pockets. The slugs are the size of quarters.

BERNIE: We've been putting these in the video games at Marshak's Arcade. The machines think they're quarters, but they're not. They're just metal disks my older brother makes in a metal working class he's taking. They're not worth a penny.

VINCENT: This way, we can play as many games as we want and not spend a cent of our allowance. Pretty smart, huh?

ALICIA: That's not smart. That's stealing.

KARL: It is not. What do you think we are—thieves? Now if you stuffed that sweater under your coat and walked out of the store with it, *that* would be stealing.

JANET: She's right, Karl. It is stealing. If you're not careful, you're going to get caught.

ELIZABETH: And probably end up in jail or something.

ROBYN: I don't think Bernie here would look very good in stripes.

ALICIA: Especially horizontal ones.

BERNIE: What do you mean by that?

ROBYN: That you would have to go to jail.

BERNIE: No, I mean about the stripes. Why wouldn't I look good in stripes?

ROBYN: Who said anything about stripes?

BERNIE: You did. You said I wouldn't look good in stripes. And Alicia said especially not horizontal ones.

ROBYN: Oh yes, that. Well, I just meant that stripes . . .

ALICIA: Just the horizontal kind . . .

ROBYN: Stripes that go from side to side might make you look, um, a little bit, uh . . .

BETHANY: Shorter. Horizontal stripes would make you look shorter. Not that you're short or anything. It's just that . . .

ALICIA: If you ask me, you should forget about using these slugs. You really are going to get caught. You might not get sent to jail, but you'll probably wish you had when your parents find out . . . By the way, prisoners usually wear bright orange now, not black and white stripes. Don't you watch cable?

BETHANY: Greg, I overheard your mom telling my mom that she has about had it with you.

GREG: What's my mom doing telling your mom stuff about me?

JANET: I was there, too. They were just talking about the water balloon incident. Your mom said if you ever pulled anything like that again, she was sending you to military school.

BERNIE: I wouldn't risk it, Greg. I heard the military is really big on stripes, too. You don't want to look *short*.

GREG: (*Ignoring Bernie*) Well, this whole thing is different. It doesn't involve any water balloons at all, and it definitely won't ruin anything, either. Besides, if you're so caught up in "doing the right thing," what were you doing eavesdropping on someone's conversation?

JANET: I wasn't eavesdropping. I just happened to overhear. That's all.

BETHANY: Do me a favor, Janet. If you ever just happen to overhear something, don't go repeating it to everyone, all right?

JANET: What's everyone getting mad at me for? (*She gestures to the boys.*) They're the ones stealing.

VINCENT: It's not stealing. It's just getting a free game. Those games are too short, anyway. They've been ripping off innocent kids like us for years.

KARL: They're lucky we're in their stupid arcade at all. We could just stay home and play Nintendo.

BETHANY: Well, why don't you?

KARL: (*Sarcastically*) Like I'm really going to spend all my time at home.

NARRATOR #1: The students continue talking as they walk out of the mall.

NARRATOR #2: Later that evening, Alicia is at home eating dinner with her parents and her older brother Jacob.

ALICIA: Mom, Dad—I've been wanting to bring up a small money matter with you, if you don't mind.

MR. JOHNSON: (*Sighing*) How much do you want this time?

ALICIA: It's not that much, Dad, especially if you look at it as an investment.

MR. JOHNSON: Oh, are you buying stocks and bonds now?

MRS. JOHNSON: Alicia, if this is for more clothes, the answer is "no," so just forget it.

JACOB: No kidding. We're going to have to move into a colossal edifice just to accommodate all your clothes.

ALICIA: What do you mean "colossal edifice"? Did you accidentally swallow a dictionary or something?

MR. JOHNSON: Your brother's right, Alicia. You are getting a little too interested in your wardrobe lately.

JACOB: A little?

ALICIA: It's just one sweater. That's it. I'll never ask for another thing again as long as I live. I promise. I just want to wear it to the basketball game next week. And after that, too, of course. I mean, I'll get a lot of use out of it. And you have to admit it gets pretty cold around here sometimes.

MRS. JOHNSON: Not cold enough for you to get another sweater.

ALICIA: But, Mom, you haven't even seen it. If you just come to the mall with me and look at it, you will love it, too. It sets off my eyes.

MRS. JOHNSON: I think maybe you're spending too much time at the mall. Perhaps you need to spend a little more time at home.

JACOB: Uh-oh, Alicia. I think the maternal figure in this household is implying that you ought to be grounded.

ALICIA: Since when did you start using words like "implying" and "edifice" and "maternal figure"?

JACOB: Since I started dating Joanna.

ALICIA: Beautiful Joanna with her eye on Harvard?

JACOB: You've got it. By the way, Mom, these mashed yams and cooked carrots are simply delectable. Would you mind if I just put the rest of mine in a plastic bag and shared your culinary talents with Joanna?

MRS. JOHNSON: Nice try, Jacob. Listen, Alicia, I'm warning you that if you keep asking for money every time you go to the mall, you're going to have to find something else to do with your time.

MR. JOHNSON: Speaking of the mall, did you hear Mr. Marshak down the street is offering a big reward?

JACOB: The same Mr. Marshak whose unfortunate children have my avaricious sibling as a babysitter?

ALICIA: I am not *avaricious*, whatever that means.

MRS. JOHNSON: What is he offering a reward for?

MR. JOHNSON: People have been stealing from that arcade he opened up in the mall. Instead of using quarters, they have been making metal slugs and using them in the video games. He's offering reward money to anyone who can give him information about who is doing it.

ALICIA: (*Nervously*) Why is he bothering with a reward? Some people would say that's not even stealing.

JACOB: Well, they would be stupid then. Of course it's stealing.

MR. JOHNSON: Your brother's right, Alicia. Mr. Marshak makes his living off the quarters in those games. When people play without paying, it's the same as taking money right out of his billfold.

ALICIA: (*Still nervous*) Does he, um, have any idea who's doing it?

MR. JOHNSON: No, not yet, but he's keeping an eye out for them. It has become quite a problem for his business. He has to pay for buying or renting all those machines, renting the building space, and paying employees. If everyone started using slugs in the machines, he would have no income at all.

ALICIA: I guess I never thought of it that way.

JACOB: Some people would say you never think, period.

NARRATOR #1: Before the first bell at school the following Monday morning, Alicia is discussing the reward money with her friends.

ALICIA: Do you know what the weirdest part of all this is? The reward money is exactly as much as that sweater costs.

JANET: What sweater?

ELIZABETH: Oh, no. Not *that* sweater again. You're not still thinking about it, are you?

ALICIA: Of course I am. Who could forget it? And the basketball game is this Friday, so if I'm going to get that reward money, I need to do it soon.

ROBYN: You're not actually thinking of telling on the guys, are you? Surely you're not going to get your friends in trouble just because you want to buy an overpriced sweater!

ALICIA: It's not just for the sweater. What they're doing is wrong. It's stealing.

JANET: Yes, but they're still your friends.

ALICIA: No, they're not. They're acquaintances. Acquaintances are just people you know. They're not the same as friends. And what about Mr. Marshak? He's somebody's friend. Just because he's not *my* friend doesn't mean he should keep getting ripped off. Besides, I really need the money.

ROBYN: Everybody needs the money. I could use it to buy some new CDs. Janet could use a new hockey stick. But you don't see us telling on our friends.

JANET: It's just not right to get your friends in trouble.

ROBYN: And tell me this: Were you considering telling on them before you found out the reward money was exactly as much as you needed to buy that sweater?

ALICIA: Well . . . I don't know. I mean, there was such a short amount of time between when I saw the sweater and when I heard about the reward.

BETHANY: I can't believe you're thinking of telling on Greg Sanders. You've had a crush on him since grade school. I can't figure out why, but you have.

JANET: You used to put love notes in his Power Rangers lunch box.

BETHANY: And in his Ninja Turtle coat pocket.

ROBYN: And in his Batman pencil box.

NARRATOR #2: As the girls go on with their list, the bell rings, and everyone leaves for class.

NARRATOR #1: By noon the next day, Alicia has decided what to do about her problem. As she sits alone in the library after lunch, Greg Sanders sits down next to her.

GREG: Hey, Alicia, what's going on? Where are the rest of your friends?

ALICIA: I'm not sure. I told them I had to finish some homework.

GREG: Me, too. . . Hey, are you going to the basketball game on Friday? It would be cool to see you there—if you're going, I mean. I might actually get to play this time.

ALICIA: Really?

GREG: Yes. I've been practicing pretty hard . . . Did you ever get that sweater you wanted at the mall?

ALICIA: You remember that sweater?

GREG: Yes. Didn't it have a lot of red in it?

ALICIA: It did . . . Greg, I need to tell you something, and I don't want you to get mad at me, okay?

GREG: Well, what is it?

ALICIA: Promise you won't get mad.

GREG: How can I do that when I don't know what you're going to say?

ALICIA: Just promise, okay?

GREG: Well, all right, all right. I promise.

ALICIA: Okay. You know Marshak's Arcade? Well, Mr. Marshak lives down the street from me, and he knows someone's been using fake coins to play the video games. He's offering a reward to anyone with information about it.

GREG: Hey, you're not going to tell, are you?

ALICIA: It doesn't matter who tells. If you keep this up, you're going to get caught.

GREG: Well, it's not like this is any of your business, but we stopped using the slugs.

ALICIA: You did?

GREG: Yes, Bernie's brother told my brother David what he was doing for us. David got mad and said he wasn't giving me a ride to school anymore if I kept using the slugs. He called me a thief. Can you believe that?

ALICIA: Well . . .

GREG: And then Bernie bailed out of the deal. He was joking around about not wanting to wear horizontal stripes, but I think he felt bad about Mr. Marshak. He told me Mr. Marshak used to buy lemonade from him every time he set up a stand when he was a little kid—even if it was the middle of winter. So are you going to tell on us?

ALICIA: No, not if you and the rest of the guys go tell him you were the ones cheating him.

GREG: (*Laughing*) Right. I'm going to stop, but I'd be nuts to tell him I was doing it before!

ALICIA: You ought to pay him the money you owe for all those games then.

GREG: It's probably just a few dollars.

ALICIA: So?

GREG: Well, there are limits.

ALICIA: Why? If you think it's just a few dollars, then you ought to pay him a few dollars.

GREG: I'll think about it, okay? But only anonymously.

ALICIA: Seriously?

GREG: Seriously.

ALICIA: Are you mad at me?

GREG: Yes.

ALICIA: Will you get over it?

GREG: Probably.

ALICIA: By Friday?

GREG: Maybe. Hey, you never answered my question.

ALICIA: Which one?

GREG: About the sweater. Did you get it?

ALICIA: No. My mom wouldn't give me the money. She says I have enough sweaters.

GREG: You can say that again.

ALICIA: What do you mean?

GREG: I mean I don't think I've ever seen you in the same clothes more than twice.

ALICIA: You noticed?

GREG: (*Smiling*) Yes, I noticed.

To Talk About

1. Why do the boys think it is all right to use the slugs to get free games? Why do they stop using the slugs?

2. Would Greg have stopped using the slugs if his brother had not threatened him?

3. Do you think Greg will repay Mr. Marshak for the games he didn't pay for? Why or why not?

4. List the reasons why Alicia considers turning in the boys. Which reason do you think is the most important to her? Why?

5. If Alicia hadn't known the Marshaks, would her thoughts and actions have been different, in your opinion? Why or why not?

To Write About

1. In the play, Greg is clearly the leader of his group of friends. How does a leader act? How does someone become a leader of a social group?

2. If you knew one of your friends was stealing from someone, what would you do? Would you confront him or her? Would you report your friend? Would you ignore the situation? What if your friend was stealing from you or a member of your family? Would your answer be different?

3. Alicia and her friends question Greg on the issue of stealing from the arcade, but it's not always so easy to stand up to someone in real life. What makes it sometimes hard to stand up for something you believe?

4. Is it easier to stand up for yourself or someone else? Why?

5. Early in the play, the students talk about how adults stereotype teenagers. What are some of the stereotypes adults have about teenagers? How do you think teenagers stereotype adults?

6. How can a stereotype hurt the person being stereotyped? How can a stereotype hurt the person who holds the stereotype?

7. If you were rewriting the end of the play, what would you change?

The Daily Grind

Horace Newton, the famed (and fictional) politician, is worried because there aren't enough people to work in the restaurants and stores across the United States. Therefore, he has proposed the following law: All students 12 years old and older must hold a job and work 10–15 hours every week in addition to going to school. Needless to say, his proposal has caused quite a debate. Some people think it's ridiculous. (Students have enough to do already!) Others think it is not such a bad idea. (It will keep students out of trouble and give them some spending money!)

Brainstorm at least five reasons for supporting each opinion on this (You should have 10 reasons in all, five in support of the measure and five against it.) Remember, it doesn't matter what your real opinion is at this point.

1. _____   1. _____

2. _____   2. _____

3. _____   3. _____

4. _____   4. _____

5. _____   5. _____

Now, decide what you think. Choose one of the following topic sentences:

Students 12 years old and older should be required to hold a job and work 10–15 hours every week in addition to going to school.

Students 12 years old and older should not be required to hold a 10–15-hour a week job in addition to going to school.

Now write a paragraph supporting your view. Be sure to include at least three reasons supporting your position.

_____

_____

_____

_____

_____

_____

_____

_____

Stealing or Not?

The students in the play argue about whether putting metal slugs into a video machine is actually stealing. What do you think? What *is* stealing? Look at the list of situations below and write an "S" next to the ones you think involve stealing. Write an "N" next to the ones you think do not involve stealing. Then defend your answer, in writing.

1. _____ Your friend Melanie works in an office. She doesn't think she receives a fair wage and believes the company is taking advantage of her. Every once in a while, she takes home pens, paper, notebooks, paper clips, and other office supplies to make up for what she doesn't get in her paycheck. _____

_____

_____

_____

_____

2. _____ Somehow, Heidi's television receives a cable channel she didn't order and doesn't pay for. She doesn't report this to the cable company because it was that way when she moved in. It's OK with her, though, because she likes the channel and watches it often. Besides, who has time to call the cable company and wait for someone to come out and fix every single little problem? _____

_____

_____

_____

_____

3. _____ Every afternoon after school, Zeke works as a cook at The Great Steak Out, a steak and seafood restaurant. He doesn't have much time to eat after school before heading off to work, so by the time he gets there, he is usually very hungry. The food smells so good that sometimes he cracks open some crab legs and eats them. He says the food gives him the energy he needs to work really hard, and besides, he's the one cooking it. _____

_____

_____

_____

_____

4. _____ Last year Herb's teacher loaned him a book, and he forgot to return it. Then he lost it. Now he's found it again, but he decides not to return it because his teacher has probably forgotten about it anyway. _____

_____

_____

_____

_____

5. _____ Thirteen-year-old Gretchen looks a lot younger than she is. When she goes to the movies and the cashier charges her for a less expensive "12 and under" ticket, she doesn't say anything. _____

_____

_____

_____

_____

6. _____ Your cart at the grocery store is squeaky and won't turn properly. When you bend down to jiggle the annoying little wheel that's causing you all the trouble, you spot a $20 bill just lying on the floor. You pick it up, stuff it in your pocket and then donate it to the guy ringing the bell for charity outside the store.

_____

_____

_____

7. _____ Instead of buying a CD you want, you make a recording of your friend's copy.

_____

_____

Now define stealing. In your opinion, what is it? Pretend you are trying to explain it to someone who has never heard the word before.

_____

_____

Look back at your answers to items #1–7. Are your answers consistent with your definition of stealing? In other words, do your opinions fit your definition? Explain.

_____

_____

Hanging Out at the Mall

Young people are important to advertisers. That's because they have a relatively large amount of money to spend. Think about it. Unlike most adults, teenagers usually don't have to pay rent or buy their own food or other basics. Instead, they get to spend their money on all kinds of other things—fun things—like movies, music, fast food, and clothes. Teenagers spend billions of dollars every year, and advertisers are keenly aware of this fact.

With all their spending power, teenagers have a huge influence on some very large companies. Imagine what would happen, for example, if the whole teenage population decided not to buy music anymore. The effects would be enormous.

Imagine that you could create a business that would appeal mainly to teenagers. It might be a business at your local mall, an Internet business, or some other kind of business. What would you sell? How would you advertise? What hours would you be open? What else would you do to attract young people to your store? Who would you hire? Describe the business you would create.

_____

_____

_____

_____

_____

_____

_____

_____

_____

_____

_____

_____

_____

_____

_____

_____

_____

_____

Election Day Blues

CHARACTERS

Narrator #1
Narrator #2
Ms. Matthews
Mr. Kain
Principal Wiggins
Mrs. Cornwall
Ms. Salinas
Molly

Students (male):
    Bernie
    Ryan
    Martin

Students (female):
    Jade
    Sonya
    Elizabeth
    Paige
    Kelly

NARRATOR #1: A small group of students is sitting around a table at a fast food restaurant, right after the Morrisey School evening band concert.

NARRATOR #2: One of the girls, Jade, is complaining about her mother, who, at the last minute, could not attend Jade's band concert because of a severe headache.

JADE: How could she do this to me? And the one time I was good enough to get a solo, too.

SONYA: Oh, Jade, would you quit feeling sorry for yourself? Your mom's one of the coolest people I know over the age of 20.

JADE: (*Ignoring her*) You know, they have a word for parents like her: *unsupportive!* My mother is the most unsupportive person I know. I'm probably going to end up in prison eating wormy tacos, and it will be all her fault for never being there for me. That will show her.

ELIZABETH: Stop being so dramatic, Jade. She had a headache.

SONYA: Yes, I don't know about you, but if I had a headache, I sure wouldn't want to go sit in the bleachers of some school gym and listen to Bernie blast away on his tuba. In fact, I wouldn't want to do that even if I didn't have a headache. No offense, Bernie.

BERNIE: Would you stop doing that, Sonya? You always say something mean and then say "no offense" right after it, like that's supposed to make it OK.

SONYA: (*Ignoring Bernie*) All I'm saying, Jade, is that your mom's not so bad. Think about all those times she drove us to the mall when she could have made us walk. If I'd had to walk all that distance in the rain last week, my hair would have been so frizzy. Sort of like Paige's hair is today.

PAIGE: Is it possible for you to say one complete sentence without insulting someone?

ELIZABETH: Jade, how about when your mom helped us with that second batch of cookies after we burned the first batch? Even your dog wouldn't eat them.

SONYA: Yes, not even Bernie would have eaten those cookies. No offense, Bernie.

BERNIE: Whatever you say, Sonya.

KELLY: (*Changing the topic*) So, Jade, what's our next step for showing Martin Foster what's what and winning that student council race?

JADE: I don't know. That's another thing that's got me down.

SONYA: Not to be mean or anything, but it does look like just about everybody in school is going to vote for him instead of you.

JADE: (*Sighing*) Did you see Martin at lunch today? He was passing out custom-made pens with the words "Foster's your man" written on the side. He had special buttons made too, with his picture on them. He's even passing out those silly straws with all the loops in them. I guess he wants the class clown vote, too.

SONYA: Oh, don't worry about that. Bernie won't vote for him, will you Bernie?

RYAN: (*Interrupting before Bernie can answer*) Wow, Martin must be spending a fortune! How are you going to compete with custom-made silly straws, Jade? You should give us all T-shirts. I'd vote for you for sure if you gave us T-shirts, especially if they were cool ones.

JADE: (*Sarcastically*) Gee, thanks, Ryan. What color would you like? (*To everyone*) Actually, I'm thinking of dropping out of the race. Martin Foster's pretty popular, and he's getting more so with every button, pen, and silly straw he hands out.

SONYA: I have an idea. How about if we stop trying so hard to depress ourselves and talk about something more cheerful? Did you hear we might get to go to New York for the band and choir competition?

KELLY: New York—as in the city or the state?

SONYA: As in the city! New York City! As in Broadway! As in Forty-Second Street!

RYAN: Did you hear how much it's going to cost, though? Five hundred dollars a person. My parents will never spring for that.

JADE: (*Still depressed*) My mom could never afford that, either. But I bet Martin Foster's parents can.

ELIZABETH: Yes, Martin will probably be the only kid who gets to go. He'd better start working on a solo.

SONYA: (*Sarcastically*) Well, you guys have been so much fun that I absolutely hate the thought of leaving, but I have to write that paper for Mrs. Carson on the Great Depression. Maybe that will cheer me up. See you tomorrow.

NARRATOR #1: After Sonya leaves, everyone decides to head home.

NARRATOR #2: When Jade walks into her house, her mother and 9-year-old sister, Molly, are waiting up for her, working on her campaign posters.

MS. MATTHEWS: How was the concert, honey? I wish we could have been there. Did you get through that tricky part of your solo?

JADE: (*Softening*) Yes, it went pretty well. Sonya said it brought tears to her eyes, but you know how dramatic she can be.

MOLLY: Yes, remember when she sang "Best of Friends, Best of Times" outside the window on your birthday, and all the dogs on our whole street started howling?

JADE: I remember. Listen, Mom, about these campaign posters . . .

MOLLY: You don't like them, do you? I told Mom they should have been on purple paper instead of green, but nobody ever listens to me. I'm just the kid sister. Wait until I turn 10, though. Then you'll have to listen to me.

JADE: (*Annoyed*) Why? What's so special about 10? I never understand your weird logic. (*Shaking her head and getting back to the subject*) Anyway, I don't think I'll be needing the posters because I'm thinking of dropping out of the race.

MS. MATTHEWS: Oh, really? Why?

JADE: The guy I'm running against is putting a lot of money into customized buttons, pens, silly straws, and who knows what else.

MOLLY: What does "customized" mean?

MS. MATTHEWS: It means he spent a lot of money on something people will use once and then throw away.

JADE: He's been passing them out every day at lunch, and I think people are falling for it. I think they're actually going to vote for him just because of those stupid trinkets.

MOLLY: Are silly straws those straws with all the neat loops in them that I always ask for and you never buy me?

MS. MATTHEWS: Yes. I never buy them for you because you don't need them. And neither do those kids at school. Jade Gertrude Matthews, I never want to hear you sound so hopeless again. Silly straws are the silliest reason in the world to give up on something you want so badly. Who needs such things? What you need to do is think of something the students really want and figure out how to get it for them. Maybe it's a longer lunch break or something, I don't know.

JADE: I don't know, either.

MOLLY: I don't know, either.

MS. MATTHEWS: You know your friends, don't you? What do they want? They're normal kids.

MOLLY: No, they're not.

MS. MATTHEWS: Well, mostly normal. What do they really need?

NARRATOR #1: Right then, Jade gets an idea. Three weeks later, every band and choir member in school is in a paved parking lot washing cars to raise money for the trip to New York City.

ELIZABETH: Wow, Jade. This was a great idea. Look at all the cars. And have you ever in your whole life seen Bernie work so hard?

JADE: I know. It looks like he's found a hidden talent for washing tires.

RYAN: And Sonya seems to have found one for advertising.

ELIZABETH: Yes, you should have seen her earlier. She convinced the whole woodwind section to do the macarena for the people waiting in the car wash line.

KELLY: Well, it must have worked. Look at all those cars. They're backed up clear around the block.

JADE: I just hope this whole thing pulls in enough money for us all to go to New York.

PAIGE: I know. A lot of people told me they won't be able to go unless it does.

RYAN: Hey, look! There's my dad. Oh, no. He's wearing his orange T-shirt with the lawn mower on it. (*Embarrassed*) Oh, man, he's coming over here. He's actually going to talk to me while he's wearing that thing. Quick! You guys are taller than me. Stand in front of me and maybe he'll think I'm not here.

NARRATOR #2: Although Jade, Kelly, and Elizabeth move quickly to stand in front of Ryan, his father sees him and comes over.

MR. KAIN: Ryan! Hey there, buddy, how's the car wash going? Looks like you're doing a pretty good business here.

RYAN: (*Trying to be polite*) Hi, Dad. What are you and Mom doing here? I thought you were working on the yard today.

MR. KAIN: You didn't think we'd miss out on a car wash, did you, son? Especially when it's for such a good cause. And are these all the girlfriends you're always talking about?

NARRATOR #1: After Ryan's dad has sufficiently embarrassed him, he ambles back to his car and waits his turn for the car wash. Red-faced, Ryan turns to the girls.

RYAN: How could he do that to me?

ELIZABETH: (*Obviously joking*) Maybe he's got some evil scheme, some wicked agenda for ruining your life. I bet he's been plotting that move for weeks.

RYAN: (*Taking her seriously*) He's probably getting back at me for not picking up the grass clippings the last time I mowed. That's why he wore the lawn mower T-shirt. It was a sign. Otherwise he would have worn the one he got free with the new washing machine. That one's a lot worse. Even my mom acts like she doesn't know him in that one.

ELIZABETH: Ryan, I was just kidding. He's not so bad.

KELLY: (*Seeing Martin Foster approach*) Uh-oh. Look who showed up. The king of silly straws himself. What's he doing here?

JADE: Probably passing out more straws. He's determined to beat me out of the election and be the class president.

NARRATOR #2: Jade is right. Martin is passing out silly straws. When he's just about out of them, he walks over to where Jade and her friends are standing.

MARTIN: Hey, what are you all just standing around for? Aren't you the one who organized this thing, Jade? Shouldn't you at least be holding a hose or something?

JADE: For your information, Martin, I did organize this fund-raiser. I just happen to be on a break, but it looks like my time's almost up. Bye.

MARTIN: So what's your excuse, Ryan? How come you're goofing off? Are you on a "break," too?

RYAN: Yes, and it's just about over.

MARTIN: Ryan, I'm sorry. I don't know why I said that.

RYAN: Maybe because you're a jerk.

MARTIN: Hey, I said I was sorry. All I meant was . . .

NARRATOR #2: Martin doesn't get to finish his apology before Ryan walks away.

NARRATOR #1: The car wash ends with only a minor water fight, and by the following Monday, Jade has turned the money over to Principal Wiggins to count.

NARRATOR #2: Seated in their homeroom class, the students listen to Principal Wiggins read the day's announcements over the intercom.

PRINCIPAL WIGGINS: (*Being very jolly*) Good morning, students! And what a beautiful morning it is! The sun is shining. The birds are singing. We're getting three new computers for the media center! And now for a big announcement: Thanks to all of you who helped with the car wash this weekend. Because of your efforts, the band and choir will be taking a 4-day trip to New York City.

NARRATOR #1: The whole class cheers.

RYAN: All right, Jade! Way to go!

PRINCIPAL WIGGINS: All righty. Before I get on with the next item of business, here's Mrs. Cornwall, everybody's favorite school cook. What are we having for lunch today, Mrs. Cornwall?

MRS. CORNWALL: Well, in keeping with my new gourmet lunch menus, today we are having salmon pizza, made with unbleached flour, of course, and with gorgonzola cheese.

NARRATOR #2: The whole class groans.

MRS. CORNWALL: And for those of you who have been using the white sauce to plaster your eggplant croquettes to the bottoms of the tables, you can expect some pretty hefty detention time when we find out who you are.

BERNIE: (*Guiltily*) Uh-oh.

PRINCIPAL WIGGINS: Thank you, Mrs. Cornwall. Be sure to save a slice of that unbleached salmon pizza for me. I'm sure it will go fast. Now, I want to remind everybody to stop by the cafeteria today and vote for next year's student council officers. (*Very seriously*) As you well know, a person who doesn't vote has no right to complain about the way things are run. By the way, tell your parents that, too. My brother is running for city council next month . . . Thank you, students. Have a great day.

SONYA: Can you believe it's finally here, Jade?

ELIZABETH: It's here. By the time you leave school today, you will know if you're the new class president.

SONYA: Oh, Jade, I'll be so proud of you. Before you know it, you'll be President of the United States. Will you let me sleep in the Lincoln bedroom?

KELLY: Sonya, you're a very strange person.

JADE: It's kind of weird. Even though I feel sick to my stomach thinking about when the results will be read, I'm glad I stayed in the race. Well, I *think* I am, anyway.

BERNIE: It sounds to me like you've got a pretty good chance. A lot of our class is in either band or choir, and they're all pretty excited about going to New York. They wouldn't get to if it weren't for you.

PAIGE: Yes, I was talking to Chet Stevens, and he said if he was in our class, he would definitely vote for you. He said the way you planned that whole car wash and everything was great.

SONYA: (*Suspiciously*) What were you doing talking to Chet Stevens? I told you a week ago that I like Chet Stevens. Remember? Are you trying to move in on Chet behind my back?

ELIZABETH: Sonya, all she did was talk to the guy. It's not like she asked him out or anything.

PAIGE: Right. It's not like I asked him out or anything . . . Except that maybe I kind of did. But not really. We're just going for a walk. No big deal.

SONYA: (*Surprised*) I can't believe that you, of all people, would do this to me. You, my best friend. Except for Jade, of course. And maybe Kelly.

KELLY: What do you mean, "maybe Kelly"? Who carried your bass drum to school for you every day for a month when you broke your leg?

JADE: Would you guys please stop it? I'm the one with the stomachache. I'm the one who has to walk around all day looking everybody in the face and wondering if they voted for me.

SONYA: You're right, Jade. I guess we can put our differences aside for one day for a dear, dear friend. At least I can, anyway. I don't know about Paige, though. She doesn't seem to know what true friendship really is.

NARRATOR #1: Just as Paige is about to defend herself, the bell rings, and the students rush off to their next class.

NARRATOR #2: Jade's next class is English, which she has with Martin Foster.

MARTIN: Hey, Jade, I know the bell's about to ring, but I just wanted to tell you that I'm sorry about the car wash. Well, not the car wash. I'm sorry about what I said at the car wash.

JADE: You mean about how you accused me of not working very hard?

MARTIN: Yes, I was kind of rude. I guess I was just nervous. I saw how hard you worked to get that whole thing together. And I knew other people must have seen it, too. I figured that after that, everyone would vote for you and you would win by a landslide.

JADE: Well, I guess we'll find out today. I'm pretty nervous.

MARTIN: Me, too. I feel sort of sick to my stomach.

JADE: I know. Are we crazy, putting ourselves out there to be judged by these people?

NARRATOR #1: Right then, the bell rings, and Jade and Martin go to their seats.

NARRATOR #2: When Jade and her friends finally meet again, it's in the auditorium, where Jade and Martin will find out which one of them will be the new class president. The opponents smile at each other as Principal Wiggins steps up to the microphone.

PRINCIPAL WIGGINS: (*Sounding kind of sick and weak*) Good afternoon, students. I hold in my hands the names of next year's student council officers. I've been feeling a little under the weather since the salmon pizza, so I've asked Assistant Principal Salinas to read the election results to you.

MS. SALINAS: Please come forward after I read your full name and the office you've been elected to hold. All right, then. Your new class secretary is . . . Andrew William Jacobs.

NARRATOR #1: The whole class cheers and applauds.

MS. SALINAS: Please hold your applause until all the names have been read. The new class treasurer is Reuben Marcos Hershey.

NARRATOR #1: The whole class cheers and applauds again.

MS. SALINAS: The new vice-president is Brian Trevor Vigil.

JADE: (*Speaking quietly to her friends*) Oh, great. It looks like everyone just voted for the boys.

BERNIE: Don't worry about it. It's probably just a coincidence.

SONYA: If you think this is just a coincidence, you've got some things to learn, Bernie. There's sexism here, and I for one, am not going to stand for it! We're going to fight this, Jade! Even if we have to go all the way to the Supreme Court!

RYAN: You should have passed out T-shirts, Jade.

MS. SALINAS: Would the students in the fifth row please be quiet so I can read the results? Now, the new class president is . . . Jade Gertrude Matthews.

NARRATOR #1: Once again, the whole class cheers and applauds.

NARRATOR #2: Jade's friends watch as she walks up on the stage to stand with the other class officers.

SONYA: Oh, I'm just so happy I could cry. It all paid off. Hand me a tissue, will you, Kelly?

KELLY: Why would I be carrying tissues around? Just use your sleeve or something.

SONYA: Are you kidding? This shirt is 100% silk.

ELIZABETH: No, it's not.

SONYA: Oh, that's right. I'm saving that one to wear tomorrow with my black skirt.

PAIGE: I've got a tissue if you want it, Sonya. I know I'm not your favorite person right now, but you can have it if you want.

SONYA: Thanks, Paige.

BERNIE: (*Interrupting*) Hey, Jade never told me her middle name was Gertrude.

ELIZABETH: She was named after her grandma.

SONYA: Poor girl. She'll never live that down once she becomes leader of the free world.

RYAN: Well, I'm glad Jade won and all, but I sure wish she would have passed out T-shirts.

To Talk About

1. When the play opens, Jade is upset that her mother did not attend the band concert. She accuses her mother of being unsupportive. Judging from the rest of the story, do you think that is true? Why or why not?

2. There is never any guarantee that Jade will win the election. What if she had lost? Do you think she would have regretted running for office? Why or why not?

3. Is Sonya a good friend? Why or why not?

4. Jade wins the election. Do you think that ending is believable? Why or why not?

To Write About

1. Sometimes people feel worse about what they did *not* do than what they did do. When have you regretted *not* choosing to do something? Explain.

2. Did you vote in the last school election? Why or why not? How did you decide who to vote for? Were there any real issues, or was the vote just a popularity contest?

3. Toward the end of the play, Sonya feels betrayed by Paige. Do you think she has good reason? Why or why not?

4. Today, any United States citizen over 18 years of age is allowed to vote. But that hasn't always been so. For example, in our country's early years, only White men who were land owners could vote. Women were not allowed to vote until August 26, 1920. Despite changes in voting rights, many people do not exercise their right to vote. In the 1996 U.S. presidential election, for example, only 49% of the voting population actually voted. What explanations can you offer for such a low turn-out? Why do you think people choose not to vote?

5. Have you ever noticed when someone starts a sentence with, "Not to be mean or anything, but . . ." the person usually does end up saying something mean? Why do you think people say mean things about others? Why do you think they use the phrase, "Not to be mean or anything"?

6. Write a different ending to the play, one where Jade loses the election.

And They All Lived Unhappily Ever After . . .

The play ends with Jade winning the election. For some reason, we all knew she would win. It could be that we are trained to expect a happy ending. The fairy tales we grew up with all had happy endings. Even the sitcoms we watch solve a problem, cheerfully wrap things up and end within 30 minutes. But, as we all know, happy endings don't always happen in real life. Perhaps that's why we enjoy happy endings in our stories, movies and television shows.

Think about Cinderella. She dazzled the prince, the shoe fit and the prince rescued her from her hard life with her wicked stepmother. What if Cinderella had broken out in pimples right before the ball? What if the glass slippers had rubbed blisters on her feet during the ball? What if the prince decided he wanted to date others before making a commitment? Some would say these scenarios would be much more like real life.

Take another fairy tale and rewrite the ending. Give it a "real life" instead of a fairy tale finish.

_____

_____

_____

_____

_____

_____

_____

_____

_____

_____

_____

_____

_____

_____

_____

Risk

Jade is taking a risk when she enters the student council race. At one point in the play, she is so worried about losing that she almost drops out of the race. What could Jade have lost by staying in the race? What could she have gained by staying in the race? What would she have definitely lost had she dropped out? What would she have definitely gained by dropping out?

It is not always a good idea to take a risk, and it's not always a bad idea. Look at the following situations that describe a risk. Think through each situation, considering the consequences of each risk, and decide whether or not each particular risk is a good idea.

1. Joe wants to go to basketball camp, but the questions on the application are difficult, and Joe doesn't like to write. He figures it will take him about 6 hours to complete the application.

    What does Joe stand to gain by completing the application?
    What does he stand to lose by completing the application?
    What will he gain by not completing the application?
    What will he lose by not completing the application?

2. Anna wants to be a part of a certain group of students at school. These students sit at the popular table at lunch, and everyone wants to be like them. Anna thinks she has a pretty good chance of being part of the group, but only if she quits the school play. She knows that this group considers drama to be a very "uncool" thing.

    What does Anna stand to gain by quitting the play?
    What does she stand to lose by quitting the play?
    What could she gain by staying in the play?
    What could she lose by staying in the play?

Answer Key

The items below are possible answers to the questions and activities in *Promise You Won't Get Mad*. These are given as samples, not as the only correct possibilities.

It's Not a Party—It's a Get-Together!

To Talk About
Page 21

1. I think Luke really does want his friends to talk him into having a party. He pretends he doesn't, but he lets them talk him into it with some pretty lame ideas. For example, no real teenager would believe that adults *want* kids to get in trouble just so that the adults won't be bored.

2. They tell him that parents expect kids to misbehave because it relieves their boredom. They also say that parents don't find out about parties kids have except in the movies. Finally, they tell him it's a get-together and not a party. The idea that it's a get-together and not a party holds the most weight for Luke.

3. Luke has a terrible time because he is worried the whole time. He is unhappy about how many people show up when they start coming into his apartment. He is also mad that Jake Vincent shows up, a boy who stole his Skittles and his Snoopy thermos in first grade. He is upset about the stain, saying his parents are going to send him to military school, or worse. He can't relax the whole time the party is going on because he's worried about his parents finding out about it.

4. Elaine tells Luke that she invited more people so he won't feel bad about being unpopular. Also, Brian invites Jennifer to the party when he sees her at the mall.

5. There would probably be more damage to the apartment in real life because there are so many people there who don't even know Luke and probably wouldn't be as careful as his friends. I think people would be more careless than they are in the play.

6. It seems like Luke is very careful to do what his parents want so he doesn't disappoint them. He also feels like they don't care about what he wants, and he feels like they abandon him when they go on their trip. He's against the party to begin with because he doesn't want to get in trouble with his parents. That shows that he tries to do what they tell him to do. He tells his friends at the beginning of the play that his parents won't take him and a friend with them on the trip, and that shows he thinks they don't care about what he wants. He says that they are "practically abandoning" him to go off on their own. Then, when Luke sees the stain, he says that his parents are going to ground him until he's dead. This shows that his parents are pretty harsh about their punishment of Luke, and that's why he's careful to do what they want.

7. I think he learns his lesson about disobeying his parents. His friends tell him that he "got all the glory" and that people will be talking for weeks about how great the party was. He loses his parents' trust, and he loses his freedom for three weeks because his parents ground him.

8. He is probably relieved because things are getting out of control and the Warrens make everyone leave. He is also not relieved because he knows that his parents are going to find out and he is going to get in trouble.

To Write About
Page 22

1. Once, I let myself be talked into leaving school to have lunch downtown with my friends, even though we weren't supposed to leave school without written permission. I knew I shouldn't go, but all my friends were going and they said we wouldn't get caught. They convinced me to go by saying that we were just having lunch, and that we wouldn't be going if the lunch at school that day were better. I went along even though I knew I shouldn't because I wanted to be with my friends. I didn't want to feel left out or have my friends call me a chicken or something.

2. My friends have a lot of influence over me, but when it comes down to it, I always think about what my parents would think if I did something. If they found out I did something wrong, they would be disappointed in me, and that would make me feel bad. But it's hard sometimes because I want to do what my friends are doing so I don't feel left out.

3. Once, there was a boy in my math class who stole the teacher's copy of a math test and made photocopies that he passed out to everyone in the class. I really wanted a copy because I'm so bad at math and I wanted a good grade on that test. My friend Stacy convinced me not to take a copy of the test. She said that if I got

caught, I'd be in big trouble. Plus, she said that it wouldn't be good in the long run because I wouldn't learn anything and I'd do a bad job on the next test, anyway. She really influenced me in a good way because I thought about it a lot and decided to get extra help for math. I did better on the next test and I didn't have to cheat! The boy got caught and suspended and everyone who cheated got in big trouble, too.

4. I don't think Luke's punishment is fair because Luke was trying his best to control the party. Plus, he felt bad about it to begin with and knew he shouldn't have a party, but his friends sort of took over. He should have been punished, but being grounded for 3 weeks and having to pay to have the whole living room carpet cleaned is not very fair.

5. I think Brian and Elaine's parents are too easy on them. Brian and Elaine don't seem upset about getting in trouble and don't seem to act like they learned anything.

6. I think Brian is most to blame because he came up with the idea in the first place. If Brian hadn't planned the party to begin with, Luke wouldn't have had a party.

7. I think grounding is fair, if it's not for too long, because being with your friends is really important and being away from them may seem unfair, but it's a good punishment. When you do something wrong and you get grounded, you learn your lesson! You can't wait for the grounding to be over, and the next time you think of doing something that will get you in trouble, you remember how bad it was not to be able to go anywhere or talk to any of your friends, and you think twice about doing something wrong.

8. Young people think if they're really careful and if they plan everything just right, they can trick their parents and have a party without them finding out about it.

9. I don't think it's realistic that Brian and Luke's parents don't check with each other about the overnight plans. It's not realistic because most parents know that that's the oldest trick in the book. I think that parents always check anyway, just to make sure it's okay with the other parents that their kid stays over.

10. I think the play is pretty close to real life, but if I had to change one thing, it would be that more damage would be done to Luke's apartment than one purple stain. Kids get rowdy when they get together, and there are a lot of people at that party.

Euphemisms
Page 23

1. Hannah cheats.
2. Joshua won't shut up.
3. Katy is a show off.
4. Andrew daydreams too much.
5. Wendy breaks the rules.

1. This food is a little overcooked. (Did you torch this hamburger with dragon's breath?)
2. Your car is an interesting color. (That car is the ugliest car I've ever seen.)
3. You look a little tired. (You look like you just crawled out of a trash can.)

A Good Argument?
Page 24

Statement: Everyone should own a ferret.
Argument: If everyone had ferrets, they wouldn't own dogs. Then nobody would have to hear dogs barking at night, or worry about getting attacked by dogs.

Statement: Everyone should have to ride the bus.
Argument: If everyone rode the bus, there wouldn't be any car accidents, pollution, or traffic jams.

Statement: All teenagers should get big allowances.
Argument: If all teenagers got big allowances, they would buy more stuff and improve the economy.

That Only Happens in the Movies
Page 25

1. Movies: People always trip and fall when they're running away from some maniac in the woods.
   Real life: People running away from maniacs in the woods would probably be more careful. Besides, people don't often have to run away from maniacs in the woods in the first place.
2. Movies: There's always a happy ending.
   Real life: There are loose ends in real life—everything doesn't resolve perfectly.
3. Movies: Nobody ever has to use the bathroom.
   Real life: People use the bathroom on a regular basis.
4. Movies: People fall in love at the drop of a hat.
   Real life: Relationships take a long time to develop.
5. Movies: Everyone drives nice cars.
   Real life: A lot of people drive junkers.

If movies were absolutely true to life, they would be boring! You'd have to wait for characters to take bathroom breaks, too. At the same time, I do like movies that show real life sometimes. I don't like movies that are totally unrealistic because there's nothing for me to relate to in movies like that.

Romeo, Romeo! Wherefore Art Thy Costume?

To Talk About
Page 37
1. The students think Crystal stole the costumes because she was mad that she didn't get a part in the play. The evidence is that someone saw her hanging around the auditorium after school one day.
2. Crystal has a bad temper. She's the kind of person who gets mad easily and acts on her anger. The girls talk about how she threw Haley's jacket in the pool and also how she ripped the list of cast members off the wall when she saw that she didn't have a part in the play.
3. Mr. Slade talks about how he misplaced his car once, and how he misplaces his billfold all of the time. It's not surprising that he puts the costumes somewhere and forgets about them.
4. Haley wants revenge for what Crystal did to her jacket, it would be a good story for the paper, and the story might help them win a prize in the journalism contest.
5. Haley doesn't want to ruin Crystal's reputation if she didn't steal the costumes. She doesn't want to be sued for libel. She knows everyone will believe the story forever and always dislike Crystal, even if it proves to be false.

To Write About
Page 38
1. I played basketball in the sixth grade, but I wasn't very good at it. I just liked to be around my friends and it was fun to play. During one game, our team was losing by a lot, and everyone was really upset, including me. But my disappointment doubled when the coach said right in front of everyone, including me, "Put Laurie in. We're losing, anyway." Being Laurie, I was pretty disappointed that the only reason the coach put me in was because I was terrible and it didn't matter if I messed up because we were going to lose anyway. I was disappointed in myself for not being better at basketball. I handled it by finally realizing that I shouldn't be disappointed in myself for not being good at basketball, but should be disappointed in the coach for being a bad coach. Also, I decided to find something I was good at. I quit basketball and joined the band instead.

2. As follows:

JORDAN: Well, what do you want, Haley? I mean, it's not like anything that important ever happens around here.
KELLY: The school play opens this weekend. That's kind of important, at least for people in this school.
CRYSTAL: Everyone's always talking about that stupid play! I'm so tired of hearing about it!
HALEY: Not everyone's talking about it, Crystal.

CRYSTAL: Well, practically everyone. And I heard there are a few people who think I took the costumes! The nerve of some people! If I get my hands on them. . .

KELLY: Take it easy, Crystal, don't get so mad!

JORDAN: You were mad that you didn't get a part in the play, weren't you? That's a pretty good reason to think that you'd take the costumes.

CRYSTAL: So, you're the one who started the rumor!

JORDAN: No, I'm not, but you do have a temper, Crystal. You even admitted to it.

CRYSTAL: That doesn't mean I stole the costumes! You people are so unfair! Goodbye and good riddance!

3. As follows:

MR. SLADE: Tyson, run out to my car and grab the box of tissues off the front seat. I can't take this scratchy bargain tissue the school buys any longer.

NARRATOR #2: Pleased to leave the tense auditorium, Tyson drags Tara with him and runs out to Mr. Slade's car.

TARA: It feels good to get out of there for a minute.

TYSON: Yes. If you ask me, Jessica and Rob should have both been kicked out a long time ago.

TARA: No kidding! They're like spoiled celebrities!

TYSON: Hey, look, there's Crystal! Let's duck behind this car.

TARA: What is she doing?

TYSON: It looks like she's going to her car. Let's get a closer look.

NARRATOR #1: Tyson and Tara sneak behind some cars so they have a better view of Crystal. They watch as Crystal takes the missing costumes out of the trunk of her car and makes her way to the auditorium.

TYSON: Oh, wow! Crystal did steal the costumes, after all!

TARA: But why is she returning them?

TYSON: I don't know. Maybe her guilt got the better of her. Let's go tell Haley and the rest of the newspaper staff that they can print their story!

NARRATOR #2: Meanwhile, back in the auditorium, Crystal comes in with the costumes.

CRYSTAL: Mr. Slade, here are the costumes. I had them dry cleaned like you asked. Sorry it took so long, but my dry cleaner is really busy this week.

NARRATOR #1: Mr. Slade, Jessica, and Rob look on with surprise as Crystal makes her way up the aisle.

MR. SLADE: Oh, yes, that's right! I can't believe I forgot that I asked you to have them cleaned! How silly of me. And here we were, thinking they were missing.

JESSICA: Mr. Slade, you mean to tell us that Crystal had the costumes this whole time because you asked her to clean them?

MR. SLADE: Well, yes, Jessica. I have a lot of things on my mind for the play, so when Crystal offered her help, I took it.

CRYSTAL: Why does everyone look so shocked? You didn't know I had the costumes?

ROB: We thought someone stole them.

CRYSTAL: Why would anyone steal the costumes? Well, when I found out I didn't have a part in the play, I really wanted to be involved, anyway, so I asked Mr. Slade if I could help.

JESSICA: Well, that was sure nice of you, Crystal.

NARRATOR #2: Finally, the opening night of the play arrives. The play is a success. Afterwards, some of the students are standing around talking.

JORDAN: So, I read in the school newspaper that Crystal was the one who stole the costumes.

ANGIE: Yes, Tara and Tyson caught her red-handed!

BERNIE: Did she get in trouble?

JORDAN: I don't know. I haven't heard anything about that.

NARRATOR #2: Rob and Jessica come running up in their costumes.

ROB: Wait! You guys are all wrong! Crystal didn't steal the costumes.

JESSICA: That's right. We were there when she brought them into the auditorium.

ANGIE: But we know what we read in the paper.

HALEY: Yes. I wouldn't have printed that story without witnesses, and I had two—Tara and Tyson.

BERNIE: We read the story. Tara and Tyson confirmed it!

JESSICA: It may have looked like Crystal was returning the costumes that she had stolen, but in fact, she was having them dry cleaned.

JORDAN: Why would she dry clean the costumes that she had stolen in the first place? That seems like a waste of money.

ROB: No, no, no! She asked Mr. Slade if she could help with the play, and he put her in charge of having the costumes cleaned.

JESSICA: And you know Mr. Slade. He just completely forgot about it!

BERNIE: What about the story in the paper?

ANGIE: So, Crystal didn't steal the costumes?

JESSICA: You guys shouldn't believe everything you read. And you, Haley, should make sure your stories are true before you print them.

HALEY: I know that. But I guess I figured two witnesses were good enough. I guess what you see isn't always what it seems, either. I'll be more careful in the future.

ROB: Hey, can Crystal sue you for libel?

HALEY: I'm going to print an apology to Crystal in the next issue.

JORDAN: Getting sued for libel would make a great story for the school newspaper.

JESSICA: Can you imagine if she did sue? I can see it now: "Newspaper staff gets sued for libel." How funny!

HALEY: Yes, really funny, Jessica, really funny.

4. My sister accused me of looking at her diary once, because it wasn't where she thought she had left it. What really happened is that our brother had been reading it. I felt bad because she thought that I was the one before she even asked our brother. I told her that I would never look in her diary, and then we bought a lock for it together so our brother couldn't look at it again.

Responsibilities
Page 39

Cab Driver

Obvious responsibilities:
Picking up people who need rides
Knowing the best way to get somewhere
Putting gas in the cab
Driving safely

Not so obvious responsibilities:
Being strong enough to lift suitcases
Knowing how to converse with people
Being polite to customers, even rude ones
Returning stuff left in the cab

Dog Walker

Obvious responsibilities:
Taking dogs for walks
Cleaning up after dogs
Keeping dogs on leash
Picking up and returning dogs to their homes

Not so obvious responsibilities:
Being strong enough to control dogs
Understanding dog behavior
Knowing good places to walk dogs
Liking dogs

Teacher

Obvious responsibilities:
Teaching students new things
Grading students' homework
Getting students to pay attention
Planning lessons

Not so obvious responsibilities:
Getting along with other teachers
Remembering kids' names
Talking with parents
Having a sense of humor

Babysitter

Obvious responsibilities:
Watching kids
Knowing where to call parents
Feeding kids
Making sure the kids are safe

Not so obvious responsibilities:
Liking little kids
Knowing games that kids like to play
Being honest and not stealing stuff
Being polite to parents

House Painter

Obvious responsibilities:
Preparing houses for painting
Painting window trim
Covering areas that shouldn't be painted
Cleaning brushes when through

Not so obvious responsibilities:
Knowing where to get paint
Not getting paint on furniture or bushes
Understanding the different types of paint
Knowing painting techniques

Chef

Obvious responsibilities:
Preparing food properly
Following recipes
Keeping the kitchen clean
Cooking what customers like

Not so obvious responsibilities:
Reading the orders correctly
Knowing what ingredients to use
Getting along with food servers
Planning menus in advance

That's What You Think
Page 41

1. What really happened is that the Dad ate some of the cake. The little brother was eating a brownie he got at school and brought home in his lunch box.

2. What really happened is that after the big bike race, Carlos was staring at the girl he really likes while he was walking his bike back to his Dad's truck. He wasn't watching what he was doing, so he stubbed his toe on a large rock that just happened to be in his way.

Our mailman always drops off our morning newspaper on our front porch, right next to the potted palm. One morning, our newspaper was not by the plant on the porch, so we thought that our mailman had forgotten to drop off our newspaper. What really happened was our dog, Bozo, picked up the paper in his mouth and carried it to the backyard, where he hid it under the honeysuckle bush.

Urban Legends
Page 42

What makes the story about the guy who had his kidney stolen believable is that some people will do almost anything for money. This urban legend addresses the human worry of having things stolen from you.

The cookie legend is very believable because stores do overcharge people sometimes, and it wouldn't be hard for the customer to send the recipe to all her friends to get revenge. It addresses the fear that people might try to rip you off.

The story about the poisoned envelopes is believable because there could be some chemical mess-up at a factory that made the glue poisonous. This legend addresses the fear that someone in a factory could make a mistake like that and not tell anyone so they wouldn't get in trouble.

I've heard an urban legend about someone finding a tarantula in some bananas at a grocery store. There's also the one about the guy with a hook for a hand, who escapes from a prison and attacks a couple who are listening to a radio announcement about that same guy. I can't think of any others, but I'm sure lots of things I hear are urban legends, but I just don't realize it.

Foreshadowing
Page 43

1. Evidence against Jill's sister: The ants are following a trail of sticky caramel.
   Foreshadowing: Earlier in the story, Jill gets angry with her sister for dropping her caramel apple on the floor.
2. Evidence against Jill's sister: The ants are heading toward a crust of bread.
   Foreshadowing: Earlier in the story, Jill's sister is watching TV and eating a peanut butter and jelly sandwich.
3. Evidence against Jill's sister: The ants are following a trail of raisins.
   Foreshadowing: Earlier in the story, Jill's sister is eating a box of raisins and keeps dropping them on the floor.

Promise You Won't Get Mad

To Talk About
Page 54

1. The boys say it's all right because the games are too short and the people who make the video games have been ripping kids off for years. Bernie's older brother tells Greg's older brother that he is making the slugs and Greg's brother David gets mad. Then Bernie stops using them.
2. I don't think Greg would have stopped because he seems to shrug it off when Alicia asks him to pay back Mr. Marshak.
3. I don't think Greg will repay Mr. Marshak, unless his friends convince him to. He just doesn't think it is that big a deal.
4. She feels bad for Mr. Marshak, and she wants the reward money to buy the new sweater. Getting the reward money to buy the new sweater is the most important reason. She talks about getting the sweater all through the play.
5. I don't think it would have made a difference if Alicia hadn't known the Marshaks. I think she just wanted the reward money.

To Write About
Page 55

1. A leader is someone who is very confident and knows how to make fast decisions that are for the best. I think that people who are leaders of social groups just naturally have the qualities that make others depend on them and listen to them.
2. I think that I would confront my friend first, and talk to him about it. It would be hard to report him, so I would just ask him to stop and if he didn't, then I would tell him that I'm going to report him even if I didn't. That might scare him into stopping, but then again, he might not be my friend anymore if I threaten him. That's a tough question. I would definitely not be his friend if I found out he was stealing from me or a member of my family. I would probably report him if he didn't give back whatever he stole.
3. If you're afraid that someone will disagree with you and cause others to gang up on you and make you feel bad, then it's harder to stand up for what you believe in. It's harder to stand up to a group of people who disagree with you than if you have other people on your side.
4. I think it's easier to stand up for yourself, because you can't really always speak for someone else. You don't know why the other person did what they did.
5. Adults think teenagers are wild, that they don't listen, that they don't have any goals, and that all they care about is their friends. Teenagers think that adults never want to have fun, that all they do is work, that they don't understand teenagers, and that they don't know anything about what's cool.
6. Stereotypes hurt people because they are judged before anyone even talks to them. Stereotypes can hurt people who hold the stereotypes because they can make the person avoid talking to someone or getting to know someone.
7. I think I would show the boys being punished in some way, or at least have them tell Mr. Marshak in person, or return the money anonymously.

The Daily Grind
Page 56

For the proposal:
1. Kids will be too busy to get into trouble.
2. They will have their own money, so they can buy the $100 jeans that their dads won't buy them.
3. Kids will be less likely to steal CDs because with their extra spending money they can just buy them.
4. Businesses can pay kids less than adults so prices will be lower.
5. Kids can also save the money they make and use it for college, so the government won't have to lend them any more money.

Against the proposal:
1. Kids won't have time to finish their homework.
2. Kids will fall asleep in class because they will be so tired.

3. No one will have time to play football or act in the school play, so schools will have to cancel all extracurricular activities.
4. With extra spending money, kids will become more materialistic.
5. Kids need time to be kids.

Students 12 years old and older should not be required to hold a 10–15-hour a week job in addition to going to school. First of all, it is ridiculous to expect young people to go to school 40 hours a week and hold down a 10–15-hour a week job. That totals 55 hours, and it doesn't even take homework time into account. Most adults don't work more than 40 hours a week, so why should kids be expected to?

Scientists say that teenagers need about 10 hours of sleep a day. This would be nearly impossible with our 11-hour days, plus homework. Also many studies have shown that extracurricular activities are very good for young people, but we would have no time or energy for extracurricular activities.

It is also not a good idea for young people to have a bunch of extra money. Some teenagers can't even be responsible with their weekly allowances, let alone all the extra money that working a lot of hours would bring. Extra money can make it easier to get into trouble with drugs and alcohol, too.

Finally, and most importantly, young people should be allowed to be young. With most people living to be around 80, we will have about 60 years of our lives to hold a job. Why can't we just enjoy these few nonworking years, without politicians forcing us into labor?

Stealing or Not?
Page 57
1. S. Melanie may not get a fair wage, but that still does not give her the right to steal from the company. If she feels so wronged, she should ask for a raise or get a new job.
2. S. This is stealing, too, I suppose. It is the cable company's fault that Heidi is getting the free service, but she is still getting something that should cost her money without paying for it. It kind of seems unfair, but Heidi should still call the cable company and right the problem. Who knows? Maybe they will give her a free month or something.
3. S. Zeke may have cooked the crab legs, but he didn't buy them. The restaurant already pays him to do the cooking. It is his job to see that he has enough to eat before he goes to work. It is not the restaurant's responsibility. Plus, the restaurant makes money by selling those crab legs. With the money they make from selling crab legs and other food, they pay Zeke. So it really isn't smart of Zeke to eat the profits.
4. S. At first, when Herb lost the book, it probably wasn't stealing because it wasn't on purpose. It was stealing though, once he found the book and he didn't return it.
5. S. Even though Gretchen doesn't "tell" them she is only 12, she lets them believe that. She doesn't tell a lie, but she allows them to believe something that isn't true. That is lying, too. This lie allows her to get in at a cheaper price, so it is stealing.
6. N. This isn't stealing, but not just because you gave it to charity. You found the money; you didn't take it. Plus, there is no way to trace cash. There would be no way to know who the money belongs to, so you really couldn't give it back to them. It was just your lucky day.
7. S. This is stealing because musicians make their money from CDs. When I record my friend's CD instead of buying my own, the musician does not get paid for the music that I now own.

Stealing is a lot of things. Stealing is when you take something that is not yours. It is when you take something that you should have paid for. It is when you find a way to get something for free or a cheaper price that is dishonest. I think my definition of stealing perfectly fits my answers above.

Hanging Out at the Mall
Page 59
Chances are if you are a teenage girl you have raided your girlfriends' closets, swapped clothes with your sister, or at the very least, coveted your best friend's designer jeans—the kind your dad says cost entirely too much. I would start a business based on this idea. I would even call it "The Closet." The Closet would be a store where teenage girls could sell their old clothes, the clothes that just sit in their closet never worn or just clothes that they are tired of or that don't fit anymore. After washing and pressing them, I would put these clothes out in the store to be sold. I wouldn't just take anyone's old clothes, however. I would only purchase clothes that fit what is "in" or

what I know my customers are looking for. This is how it would be different than your basic second-hand store. A teenage girl could even go to the mall in a great outfit, then come to The Closet and basically trade in what she was wearing for an even better outfit.

Instead of separate fitting rooms, I would have one large communal fitting room that would be like a teenage girl's bedroom complete with cushy furniture, hunky guy posters and teen fashion magazines. I would hire some teenage girls to work in the fitting room, so that customers wouldn't have to bother with hanging up the clothes that they don't want.

Of course, all of my employees would have to have a good fashion sense, so that they could recommend stuff and help customers make decisions. That's why all of my employees would have to be teenage girls. Who knows more about adolescent fashion trends than they do?

In the back of the store would be a little room called The Attic, and this is where all of the vintage clothing would be. As anyone in fashion knows, styles move in cycles, so there is always something retro in current fashion. And nothing is worse than paying $80.00 at the Gap for replicas of your mom's old clothing. To top everything off, I would have a mini-coffee bar in the corner of the store to encourage people to just hang out in the store and try on clothes.

Election Day Blues

To Talk About
Page 69

1. Jade's mother is definitely supportive because her mother helps her make campaign posters and convinces her to stay in the election race.
2. Jade probably wouldn't have been too upset if she had lost. She would have thought that it wasn't her, but the fact that Martin bought his votes. I don't think she would have regretted it because she still did a good thing by having the car wash and raising money for the trip to New York.
3. I don't think Sonya is a good friend. She seems really snotty and is always insulting everybody. For example, she says she wouldn't want to listen to Bernie play his horn and that Paige's hair is frizzy. Then she says no one is going to vote for Jade.
4. I don't think it was realistic, because there can't be that many people in the band and choir! Jade is losing, and then a few days later she wins. That's kind of hard to believe, but I guess elections can go like that sometimes.

To Write About
Page 70

1. I had a chance to go listen to an orchestra with my parents because they had an extra ticket, but I thought it would be boring, so I said "no." I regretted it because some of my friends also went and said it was really fun. It was a Christmas concert, and they had a guest singer everyone says I would have really loved.
2. Yes, I voted in the school election. I voted because some people can do a better job than others and those people should get elected. I voted for them based on what they were going to do, but sometimes I voted just because they were my friends. I think it was mostly a popularity contest, but there are some people I just wouldn't vote for even though they were my friends, because the other person was better at the job.
3. I don't think Sonya has a good reason to feel betrayed, since she is always insulting everyone and making them feel bad about themselves. Sonya hadn't even talked to the guy or even asked him out, so why should no one else?
4. Maybe the candidates just weren't very good. Or, maybe some people are too lazy to vote. I think people choose not to vote sometimes because they disagree with all of the candidates, or their candidate didn't get nominated. Sometimes it's because people are just too lazy, or maybe too busy to vote. Maybe they don't want to wait in lines, or maybe they think that their vote doesn't make a difference.
5. I think people say mean things about others to make themselves look or feel better. They use that phrase to make it seem like they're not actually trying to be mean.

6. As follows:

ASSISTANT PRINCIPAL SALINAS: I would like to announce that the new class president is. . . Martin Foster.

NARRATOR #1: Everyone applauds except Jade and her friends sitting with her. They all watch as Martin walks up on stage to stand next to the rest of the officers.

SONYA: Well, Jade, next time you'll know what to do. I don't think you handled the election well. No offense.

KELLY: Oh, be quiet, Sonya. At least Jade tried and she didn't go around trying to buy votes.

SONYA: Of course she didn't buy votes. That's why she didn't win.

JADE: I really don't think you should have to buy your votes. School elections are just popularity contests, anyway. I'm just glad that I came up with a way to raise enough money to go to New York.

PAIGE: Yes, Jade. You're right. Your plan to raise money and the fact that you carried it out is more than Martin Foster could accomplish all year, much less in one weekend.

JADE: Thanks, Paige. You're a really good friend. I'll just have to try again next year.

SONYA: And this time we're going to make T-shirts and hand out freebies!

KELLY: Well, Sonya's obviously not listening! But T-shirts are a good idea, Jade!

And They All Lived Unhappily Ever After . . .
Page 71

The three bears came home after their long walk to find their apartment ransacked. "Oh my," said Mama Bear, "I think someone has broken into our home." Grabbing his Louisville Slugger, Papa Bear told Baby Bear and Mama Bear to wait in the hallway outside the apartment. Papa Bear slowly crept up the stairs armed with his baseball bat. Mama Bear and Baby Bear were too scared to go outside alone. Also, they never really listen to Papa Bear when he is being so bossy. They quietly tiptoed up the stairs behind the big, burly Papa Bear.

As they approached the big family bedroom, Papa Bear immediately saw the culprit. Sleeping in Baby Bear's little bed was a runaway teenage girl with a bad dye job. Goldilocks was startled awake by Papa Bear's footsteps. (He does weigh about a ton, so Papa Bear can't really sneak up on someone.) She sprang out of bed and started heading for the window. Mama Bear rushed Goldilocks and nailed her in the eyes with some pepper spray. Goldilocks was stunned by the burning in her eyes and couldn't move. Right then, Papa Bear pinned her to the ground with one paw and instructed Baby Bear to call 911.

As the cops took Goldilocks away in cuffs, she thought to herself, "I've really hit rock bottom. I'm being thrown in the slammer for sitting in someone's chair, eating some nasty porridge and sleeping in a baby's bed. I think I need to find a nice family to adopt me." After Goldilocks was gone, cops and neighbors were milling around the Bears' apartment. Papa Bear was yelling at the super to get the apartment's security system fixed. A burglar-alarm salesman was giving Mama Bear an earful, saying things like, "Can you really put a price on safety?" And Baby Bear was in the living room sucking on a lollipop and talking to the police department's crisis counselor.

Risk
Page 72

1. Joe will gain a chance to go to basketball camp, which could really improve his game and help him to maybe make varsity this year. He will also gain some practice filling out applications, which will definitely come in handy when applying for schools and jobs.

    Joe will lose the time it takes to fill out the application, which could have been spent hanging out at Sean's playing Nintendo or pool. Plus, it is not going to be a fun way to spend his time.

    Joe will gain an afternoon by not filling out the application, plus he won't suffer from the headache he is sure to get from forcing himself to write.

    Joe will lose an opportunity to go to basketball camp. He could possibly make varsity without going to camp, but it is not likely. If Sean goes to camp without Joe, he will have a week full of lonely afternoons.

2. Anna could possibly be asked to sit at the popular table at lunch, which could be very good for her future social life. This also means that she may get to actually eat more of her lunch because she won't have to sit next to Big Benny anymore. He always begs and begs until she gives him most of her lunch. Also, if Anna

quits the play, she won't have to put up with moody Mrs. Harlow, the drama teacher.

Anna will lose the chance to be in the play. Also, she won't get to hang out with her friends who are in the play and don't think that drama is such an uncool thing. Plus, if she quits, Mrs. Harlow always holds grudges and probably wouldn't let Anna be in another school play ever again. Anna also will miss the high she gets from performing in front of an audience. She truly enjoys an audience's applause.

By staying in the play, Anna will get to hang out with some of her old friends. She will get to enjoy the applause of an audience. She will get to wear a neat costume. While she may still get yelled at by Mrs. Harlow, Anna won't become her enemy for life, and she will continue to do something she has loved ever since she was 5 years old. She would also like to be a movie star someday, and being in school plays is how most actors get their start.

By staying in the play, Anna may continue to be labeled a drama-nerd by the cool kids at school and will probably never get to sit at the cool table. This also means she will have to continue sitting by Big Benny at lunch. Even though she is only in 8th grade, this could hurt her chances of going to prom with a cool hunk or becoming homecoming queen.

Printed in the United States
by Baker & Taylor Publisher Services